Seasons

Seasons

Women's Search for Self Through Life's Stages

Anita Louise Spencer

 Paulist Press   *New York/Ramsey*

Library of Congress Catalog Card Number: 81:85379

ISBN: 0-8091-2437-8

Published by Paulist Press
545 Island Road, Ramsey, N.J. 07446

Printed and bound in the United States of America

Cover and interior art by Gloria Claudia Ortìz

Contents

Acknowledgements

Writing this book has been like giving birth, with all of the accompanying labor pains. There was a great deal that I wanted to say and sometimes the thought process was painful. A number of people supported me during this gestation period and to them I give my thanks:

To my three sons, Steven, Scott and Christopher, for their never ending patience and encouragement. Their instinctive wisdom has taught me a great deal about life. They have both supported me and given me "space" when I needed it the most. My sons have shown me the truth of the words: "If you love something, set it free. If it comes back to you, it was yours. If it doesn't, it never was."

To Linden Crawforth for his love and encouragement. He has shown me that egalitarian relationships really can exist. His caring has helped me to see that the people in my life are like the pillars on my porch that I see life through. And sometimes they hold me up, and sometimes they lean on me, and sometimes it is just enough to know they're standing by.

To Dr. Peter Koestenbaum, professor of philosophy at San Jose State University, who as a teacher and a therapist facilitated and witnessed my new birth. I thank him for showing me, in his own gentle way, the incredible healing power of the therapeutic relationship.

To Kevin Gordon, theologian and psychological consultant, who as both teacher and mentor encouraged me to ask the "bigger questions" in life. It was his teaching that accelerated my personal growth and launched me into a much-needed Age Thirty identity crisis. To him I will be eternally grateful.

To Dr. Brian Hall, director of pastoral counseling at the University of Santa Clara, for having both the enthusiasm and the interest in this book about women. I am deeply indebted to him for his gentle prodding and his ever encouraging support.

Lastly, I would like to thank all my beautiful friends, who have constantly supported me. They have known me as I am, understood where I have been, accepted who I have become and still, gently, invited me to grow.

Spring and *Summer*

Introduction

The last several years have seen an increasing interest in adult development. Also, it has been only recently that society has become able to ensure that its members live out their full life span. Although society is now able to keep people healthy well after the forties, the more difficult problem relating to older adulthood is in fostering psychological well-being and providing the conditions for a satisfying, productive life.

At the same time, the rapid development of powerful technology and of cumbersome institutional structures has created a need for greater numbers of productive individuals. But the need has far outstripped our cumulative understanding of middle and older adulthood and our ability to foster life in those periods. As noted by Daniel Levinson in *The Seasons of a Man's Life:*

> A few thousand years is not enough to learn what to do with middle adulthood and with the institutions that shape its course. We are still feeling our way in the dark. As I make the shift from early to middle adulthood, the tribe offers little instruction, support or cultural wisdom. What I am losing is much more evident

1

than what I may gain. I know that a new season is coming, that my life will be crucially changed. But what are the options that await me? I get many explicit messages and vague vibrations about mortality, loss, restriction; feelings that time is running out and that I may soon die, or worse, have a life without meaning for myself or others. But I get few positive images of the middle-aged hero—the lover, friend or mentor, the person of dignity, wisdom, authority, creativeness. Where is the contemporary parallel to Abraham, Buddha or Odysseus on his midlife journey?[1]

Such comments characterize the kinds of questions today's adults are asking. Every adult is interested in knowing what it means to be an adult. What are the root issues of adult life—the essential problems and satisfactions, the sources of disappointment, grief and fulfillment? Is there an underlying order in the progression of our lives over the adult years, as there appears to be in childhood and adolescence? Questions of this kind permeate much of the modern adult's consciousness. One only has to observe the tremendous response to Gail Sheehy's *Passages* to know that this subject of adult development is extremely topical.

Only in recent years have we seen psychologists and sociologists actively studying adult development. One of the more thorough studies done on adult men was undertaken by Daniel Levinson, a professor of psychology at Yale University. His book, *The Seasons of a Man's Life*, is based on intensive, long-term interviewing of forty selected men. His forty men consisted of ten executives, ten biologists, ten factory workers, and ten novelists. From his study of these men, Levinson was able to discover and map out the first complete, detailed, authoritative account of the hidden pattern that may underlie and shape every man's life. His study demonstrated the existence of adult development—how human beings continue to change, throughout their lifetimes, according to an age-linked timetable.

Another well-known study of adult development was done by George Vaillant, as summarized in his *Adaptation to Life*. This study of 268 of Harvard's healthiest and most promising undergraduates was done in order to determine how men adapt to life. His book sets forth the conclusions of his study and poses some very fundamental questions about individual men's differences in reacting to problems.

As both a student of sociology and psychology and as an adult woman, I found both the Levinson and Vaillant studies to be of significant interest. But as I reviewed their work I kept wondering if the woman's life-cycle development would follow the same pattern as the man's. I thought about this issue at great length and talked to many women friends about this and related matters. As I pondered over my own life I saw many discrepancies between my experience and those of the men reported on in these studies. As a result, I tentatively concluded that the seasons of a woman's life would be significantly different from those of a man's life. I had the feeling that society's role-expectations of women would somehow hamper, in some significant ways, the female's life-cycle personality development.

Because of my own deep personal interest in this issue, I decided to extensively research the subject of women's development and determine just what similarities and differences may exist between women and men. Are there any significant differences between men's and women's development? If there are, what role did women's early socialization and other societal constraints play in creating these differences? What role has society played in shaping the seasons of a woman's life?

I have undertaken the project of writing this book primarily in order to further my own knowledge and to answer some crucial questions that have long interested me. But I hope that in doing so I will also have contributed something worthwhile to other women's understanding of the problems of being a female today. The questions raised herein are of profound significance for all women. In order to answer them I have surveyed all the relevant literature and have pieced together what I believe is an accurate picture of the seasons of a woman's life.

In conjunction with this I will be observing those areas of a woman's life which provide opportunities for better fulfilling her full adult potential. Hopefully, by commenting on the problems inherent in being female at each season of a woman's life, I will be providing an impetus for both personal and social change.

Background and Assumptions

In thinking about the woman's life cycle, I find the imagery of seasons to be particularly helpful. The seasons can represent a series of periods or stages within the life cycle. The process is not a simple, continuous, unchanging flow, for there are qualitatively different seasons, each having its own distinct character. Each season is different from those that precede and follow it. And to speak of seasons is to suggest that the life course has a certain shape, that it evolves in a series of definable forms. Change goes on within each season and a transition is required for the shift from one season to the next. Each season has its necessary place and contributes its special character to the whole. It is a beautiful metaphor that speaks clearly to us as women.[2]

Woman as a Social Being

In order to study the evolving life course it is necessary to place the individual (in this case the woman) in society. I wish to examine a woman's own particular engagement with her environment—her relationships, roles, involvements in this world as well as her fantasies, conflicts and abilities. I need to consider both the nature of the woman and the nature of society by looking at how history, culture and social influences have shaped the woman's life.[3]

Various aspects of the self and the world influence the formation of a life structure and shape its change over time. I will be using three perspectives in considering these life structures. These perspectives are:

1. The woman's sociocultural world, as it impinges on her, has meaning and consequences for her. To understand a woman's life, therefore, we must take into account the society in which she lives. We must place her within various social contexts (e.g., class, religion, ethnicity, family, political system, and occupational structure) and understand their relevance for her.

2. Some aspects of a woman's self are lived out, while other aspects are inhibited or neglected. "The self includes a complex patterning of wishes, conflicts, and anxieties, and ways of resolving and controlling them. It includes fantasies, moral values and ideals, talents and skills, character traits, and modes of feeling, thought and action." Part of the self is conscious, but much is unconscious. Important aspects of the self, initially formed in the pre-adult era, continue to influence a woman's life in adulthood. It is necessary to observe how the woman draws upon the self, or ignores it, in her everyday life. The self is an intrinsic element of the life structure and not a separate entity.

3. One needs to examine the woman's "participation in the world." The external world provides a landscape, a cast of characters, a variety of resources and constraints out of which a woman fashions her own life. A woman selectively uses and is used by her world, through her evolving relationships and roles as citizen, lover, worker, boss, friend, wife, mother, and/or member of diverse groups and

enterprises. Participation involves transactions between self and world. The transactions take obvious forms, but subtle meanings and feelings play an important part in them.[4]

As we analyze and describe the life structure, we must also consider the choices a woman makes and how she deals with their consequences. The most important choices in adult life have to do with family, work, friendships, religion, politics and community life. We have to consider the meanings and functions of each choice within the woman's life structure. As a component of the life structure, every choice is saturated by both self and world.[5]

As I examine the woman's life-cycle development, I will be considering as many of these issues as appear to be applicable.

This book will be premised upon Levinson's life-cycle sequence. I am using Levinson's study because it is currently the only published study of adults (adult males) that is based on empirical research. Since I wish to compare women's development with men's, it is imperative that I have a model to base this comparison on. I am assuming that the tasks he assigns to the various transition points should be essentially the same for women as for men. The following is Levinson's life-cycle framework:

Ages
17–22 Early Adult Transition
22–28 Entering the First Structure
28–33 Age Thirty Transition
33–40 Settling Down into Second Structure
40–45 Mid-Transition
45–50 Entering First Mid-Structure
50–55 Age Fifty Transition
55–60 Building a Second Mid-Structure
60–65 Late Transition

65–80 Late Adulthood

80+   Late, Late Adulthood

My decision to orient this woman's study on Levinson's life-cycle framework is based on Levinson's own hypothesis:

> This sequence of eras and periods exists in all societies, throughout the human species, at the present stage in human evolution. The eras and periods are grounded in the nature of man as a biological, psychological and social organism, and in the nature of society as a complex enterprise extending over many generations. They represent the life cycle of the species. These eras and periods have governed human development for the past five or ten thousand years—since the beginning of more complex, stable societies.[6]

If Levinson's hypothesis is correct then we can conclude that women should fit into the same basic pattern and therefore should have the same tasks to accomplish at each stage in adult development.

Levinson is not the only one who has studied adult development and found a sequential pattern to it. Erik Erikson has arrived at a similar view of the life cycle on the basis of his clinical, anthropological, historical and biographical inquiries. His ego stage of Identity vs. Identity Confusion reaches its culmination during the period that Levinson identifies as the Early Adult Transition. His stage of Intimacy vs. Aloneness starts in the early twenties and runs through early adulthood. His next stage, Generativity vs. Stagnation, starts around forty and characterizes middle adulthood, while Integrity vs. Despair is the ego state of late adulthood.[7]

Jung, Ortega y Gasset and Simone de Beauvoir, among

others, have provided similar findings that would support Levinson's hypothesis relating to life cycles. Thus, I feel that it is valid to use Levinson's life-cycle sequence in my study of women.

Goal of Personality Development

It is important to mention at this point what many psychologists consider to be the goal of personality development. The goal of human growth and development has been the encouragement of ego autonomy. Ego autonomy is a concept that means a person is able to control his or her own life by adaptive choice and independent action. With ego autonomy, one has the inner freedom to develop one's potential both emotionally and intellectually. It implies the capacity to acknowledge reality in the process of making choices, but it does not mean "adjusting" to the status quo or to a specific social milieu. Ego autonomy calls for the ability to accept interdependence with other individuals, and in the process to benefit from these dependencies rather than be crippled by them.[8]

Many psychologists believe that the most important principle involved in personality-development theory is that the individuality of every person is valuable and should be defended when it is attacked by pressures for conformity. Psychologists also emphasize the fact that we need to stress the *options* available during any person's development, especially with regard to women, who are particularly burdened by rigid institutional and societal expectations.[9]

It is the premise of this book that achieving ego autonomy should be the ultimate goal of adult development. Having in mind this premise, let us proceed to look at the seasons of a woman's life.

The Spring of a Woman's Life (Age 17–28)

The spring season elicits much imagery. We think of flowers, fun, sunshine and youth. Likewise, a woman blossoms in the springtime of her life. But before a woman arrives at her real "springtime" she must manage to work through the early transition period.

Early Transition (Age 17–22)

Levinson states: "The primary tasks of every transition period are to question and reappraise the existing structure, to explore various possibilities for change in self and world, and to move toward commitment to the crucial choices that form the basis for a new life structure in the ensuing stable period."[10]

This particular transition period is often referred to as "the identity crisis." This transition corresponds to what our culture describes as "adolescent rebellion," and to what Erik Erikson has called the fifth stage of development— "identity versus identity confusion." Erikson describes this crisis as one in which "each youth must forge for himself some central perspective and direction, some working unity, out of the effective remnants of his childhood and the hopes of his anticipated adulthood; he must detect some meaningful resemblance between what he has come to see in himself and what his sharpened awareness tells him others judge and expect him to be."[11]

It is presumed that Erikson's use of the "masculine generic" here is not meant to exclude females from the need or ability to undergo this same crisis. It is very important for a woman to successfully work through this crisis, since the evidence suggests that this crisis is more problematic for the girl than it is for the boy.

Penelope Washbourn, in her book *Becoming Woman*, points out that this particular life-crisis involves separation and rebellion from the parental home and from prescribed social roles. The young woman must leave home not only physically but also psychologically. This implies breaking with the norms and values of society and its accepted goals. As Washbourn states, "For a woman, rejecting the mother, her image, and her interpretation of the female role is the deepest and often most bitter form of rebellion. She feels guilty about her hatred toward her mother, and the social framework of our culture can intensify this guilt. Rebellion, however, has been seen by early cultures as a necessary aspect of the male's journey in search of his identity. From a psychological point of view, the spiritual journey of the male away from the parental home is interpreted as a search for his masculine identity and a rejection of the maternal world in which he grew up."[12]

Washbourn opines that a male's identity appears to be made rather than given, while a woman's identity is given in her nature and is gradually revealed to her through the stages of her sexual development.[13]

Leaving home is harder for the young woman than for

the man. For at some level the young woman knows she will need to find an identity, and this necessarily involves making a choice about that option elected by her mother—namely, childbirth.[14]

Numerous studies of early female socialization indicate that the girl will have a very difficult time achieving a sense of personal identity.

Lois Vlades Hoffman, in her article "Early Childhood Experiences and Women's Achievement Motives," states that since the little girl has (a) less encouragement for independence, (b) more parental protectiveness, (c) less cognitive and social pressure for establishing an identity separate from the mother, and (d) less mother-child conflict which highlights this separation, she engages in less independent exploration of her environment.

Hoffman believes that this results in the young woman's not developing either the skills to aid her in coping with her environment or the confidence in her ability to do so. She continues to be dependent upon adults for solving her problems, and because of this she needs her affective ties with adults. Children often have fears of abandonment even when the danger is remote. Involvement in mastery exploration and the increased competence and confidence that result help to alleviate these fears, but for girls the fears are more likely to continue into adulthood.[15]

The anticipation of being alone and unloved, then, may have a particularly desperate quality in women. Hoffman goes so far as to propose that the all-pervasive affiliative need in women results from this syndrome. Thus boys learn effectiveness through mastery, while girls are effective through eliciting the help and protection of others.[16]

In a similar vein, much research has been done on women's fear of success. Matina Horner, well known for her studies of achievement-related conflicts in women, claims that most women have a motive to avoid success, that is, a disposition to become anxious about achieving success because they expect negative consequences, such as social rejection and/or feelings of being unfeminine, as a result of succeeding.[17]

As recently as 1972 Horner was still arguing that the new freedom for women had not been effective in removing the psychological barrier in many otherwise achievement-motivated and able young women that prevents them from actively seeking success or making obvious their abilities and potential. Horner states: "There is mounting evidence in our data suggesting that many achievement-oriented American women, especially those high in the motive to avoid success, when faced with the conflict between their feminine image and developing their abilities and interests, disguise their ability and abdicate from competition in the outside world—just like Sally in the Peanuts cartoon who at the tender age of five says: 'I never said I wanted to *be* someone. All I want to do when I grow up is be a good wife and mother. So . . . why should I have to go to kindergarten?' "[18]

Much of Horner's research was done with young women in the 17–22 age group. Obviously her above-stated conclusions would indicate that girls were not working through this identity crisis in a positive manner.

Kirsten Amundsen also points out that boys and girls growing up in America receive messages throughout their education that reinforce the sex-typing started in infancy. As Amundsen says, "Society's expectations about the female role dictate to the female student that she be popular, desirable, marriageable, and able and willing to bear children. At the same time, society's dictations of what is desirable in a female preclude the development of independence of mind, intellectual inquisitiveness, assertiveness, and a drive to compete."[19]

Amundsen believes that the result of all this is confusion, ambivalence, and emotional havoc among girls with talents or intellectual abilities. She feels that the result also is a damaged self-image and a decline in self-respect among the vast majority of girls who cannot transcend the narrow stereotype of behavior prescribed for them.[20]

It does not appear that young women are having much success in meeting the "identity vs. identity confusion" that Erikson states is necessary for personality development. Keeping this in mind, let us move on to the First Adult Life-Structure.

The First Adult Life-Structure: Entering the Adult World (Age 22–28)

The balance of the springtime of a woman's life is the age 22–28 period. The four major tasks of this phase are:

1. Forming a dream and giving it a place in the life structure.

2. Forming mentor relationships.

3. Forming an occupation.

4. Forming love relationships, marriage and family.

None of these tasks can be completed in this phase, and it is a developmental accomplishment to have made even moderate progress with all of them by the early thirties. But the novice should be exploring the adult world, developing adult interests and values, making important choices with regard to work, marriage and family, and forming an adult identity.[21]

The woman at the age of around 22 finds that she has several options available to her at this point in her life. Peter Koestenbaum, philosopher, illustrates these options by using the metaphor of ancient goddesses: Hera, the Greek Olympian goddess of woman and marriage; Ceres, the Roman goddess of the growing vegetation; and Aphrodite, the Greek goddess of love and beauty.

Koestenbaum points out that one of a woman's role choices—epitomized by Hera and Ceres—is as that of homemaker. In this role she is dedicated to the production of a superlative family. She assumes responsibility for the physical and spiritual creation of successful children. She is also in charge of the establishment of a happy home atmosphere and the development of a satisfied husband. If a woman chooses this role, her goals are homemaking, marriage, companionship, security, husband, children, and the satisfying knowledge that she is fulfilling the traditional female role.

A second choice for a woman during this stage is to function in the role of a creator—but outside the home. She does this by having ambitions, seeking out éclat, dedicating herself to a profession, identifying herself with a cause, or committing herself to the fulfillment of her artistic inclinations. Koestenbaum mentions that this is the primary role that the twentieth century has opened up for women; he compares this role to the goddess Ceres because the woman's creativity is self-made rather than biological, physiological, or customary.

Third, the woman has the choice of adopting the role of Aphrodite. In this case she seeks sexual gratification, romantic first love, physical beauty, and the cynosure, power and glory that go with those aspects. She desires the supreme physical and spiritual experiences of which her feminine nature is capable.[22]

Koestenbaum believes that the problems with these role choices for women are twofold: (1) the conflicts that arise among these roles and (2) the problem of achieving fulfillment in any chosen one. Both problems are due to the fact that success in the role of marriage and family-creation is usually incompatible with genuine achievements in the role of an ambitious professional woman. "The ardors and exultations of romantic love—whose paeans poets have sung and whose details novelists have exploited—are incompatible with the arduous, inexorable, and irreversible mundane, quotidian, monotonous structures of child-bearing and homemaking. As Aphrodite, woman must have a god for her man; as Hera, she recognizes that her man is human. To her, man's divinity appears in love and man's humanity in marriage."[23]

Koestenbaum points out that not only does the woman need to manage the conflicts engendered by her new freedom and by her new knowledge about her unexplored possibilities, but that even if she can choose a particular role she still must attempt to genuinely and successfully fulfill herself in it.

The problems mentioned here seem to be unique for women. Penelope Washbourn points this out: "The psychological, economic, sexual, and physical dependency that women have on marriage within a patriarchal framework means that getting married represents a personal and social achievement for the woman, whereas for the man it belongs to 'his personal life.' "[24]

Washbourn believes that the value which our society places on a woman's fulfilling the traditional roles in marriage and in child-bearing is so minimal that the woman finds that neither the husband, the children, nor the home can provide a sense of security about her worth. For the woman, marriage really represents the resolution of one identity crisis but the beginning of another.[25]

Because of these facts, Alice Rossi concludes that "the

possibility must be faced ... that women lose ground in personal development and self-esteem during the early and middle years of adulthood, whereas men gain ground in these respects during the same years."[26]

For a woman to pursue a career is almost just as impossible a choice. It takes an unusually independent woman to transcend the obstacles placed in her way by society. Edwin Lewis, author of *Developing Woman's Potential*, believes that, ideally, a career should play an important role in the personal development of a woman in much the same way it does for a man by providing her with a means for expressing her individual potential.[27]

Lewis goes on to mention that for a woman to gain from a career the kind of satisfactions that are available to men, she must recognize that she has several handicaps to overcome. He believes that "being a woman is itself a barrier to professional advancement, first because society views her with such suspicion, and second because the characteristics which promote professional advancement are not apt to be compatible with the usual concept of femininity."[28] Also, Lewis feels that a woman who wants to get ahead must run the risk of appearing "unfeminine."

Another point Lewis discusses is the important fact that the "career woman" must also accept the reluctance of society to give her full status as a woman, since the role which is lauded by society as a woman's most important accomplishment is the role of wife and mother. As Lewis says, "People may tolerate or even love a bachelor, but the spinster is viewed with suspicion. The result is that the woman who elects to concentrate on her career and does not choose to marry finds it difficult to feel fulfilled as a person."[29]

The alternative of combining a career with a marriage produces numerous problems, especially if the wife has a better job or makes more money than her spouse. Lewis believes that it would take a very secure, self-confident husband, as well as a stable, sound marriage, in order for such a differential to be tolerated comfortably. Such marriages do exist, and many are able to work this out very well, but generally "a husband and wife are so constrained by society's traditional attitudes concerning the role of each in a marriage that it requires considerable personal strength and maturity to overcome them and to achieve a mutually satisfying relationship based on the needs of both parties."[30]

Even in a situation where the wife's job does not pose a threat to the husband's sense of worth, it is still problematic to combine both a career and a family. Wendy Steward addresses this problem as follows: "In order to integrate a family and a career, a woman requires a highly supportive interpersonal environment, greater than average personal ambition, the ability to thrive on the complexity and challenge of sequentially ordering two major priorities as become necessary without sacrificing either."[31] The task sounds rather formidable, and the chances of succeeding at both career and family seem small.

It has been suggested that perhaps the initial and critical task for a young woman who wishes to respect herself as a whole person, and seriously consider her options in regard to career and/or marriage and children involves three steps: (1) identifying with a competent older woman or family member who treats her aspirations seriously, (2) respecting and identifying with women her own age who are similarly self-involved, and (3) working out a satisfactory relationship with a man who also takes her aspirations seriously and who respects and encourages her intellect, activity, and competitiveness without being threatened.[32]

While the above are excellent suggestions they are difficult to carry out. The absence of women role-models is a serious problem for the young woman. Levinson mentions that female mentors are scarce, especially in the world of work. This is because the few women who might serve as mentors are often too beset by the stresses of survival in a work-world dominated by men to provide good mentoring for younger women.

There is the additional problem of finding a male with the qualities described above. Such men are atypical. A woman can only utilize the resources available, and if there is a paucity of women role-models and a scarcity of supportive men it will make her task of achieving ego autonomy all the more difficult.

The pertinent literature on this subject seems to support the theory that there are some unique and very special problems faced by our woman in the "springtime" of her life. In recalling the four tasks of this novice phase, as defined by Levinson, we can see just where her problems lie.

The young woman is having difficulty forming a dream that is uniquely her own, which is essentially Levinson's first task. Wendy Ann Steward has done a study, based on Levinson's theories, of the formation of the early adult life-structure in women. Her studies of women indicate that there is a significant difference, in terms of certain aspects of dream formation, between men and women. She states: "The dreams that women form tend to have a strong *relational* component, that is, becoming involved in a relationship, typically expressed in the terms of wanting to get married and have a family. In contrast, the dreams reported by most men in Levinson's sample who formed dreams tended to be more *individualized*, that is, becoming a certain kind of individual, most often expressed in terms of wanting to form an occupation."[33]

If a woman's dream is a relational one then she must be

fulfilled in relation to *him* and *his* dream and consequently must await meeting him and forming an intimate bond with him before she develops as the person whose ways of being are congruent with those of the beloved partner. Maggie Scarf comments on the problems this poses for women. She states: "If she unites herself (whether in marriage or in a non-legal but long and important sexual relationship) with a man who is a high school teacher—or lawyer—or electrician—or businessman—or actor, chef, accountant, etc., she will as a matter of course, and of exposure to his occupational community, be influenced to develop those tastes, preferences, ways of existence that make sense in his world (and are supportive of his dream for the future). Her personality, and very identity, will differentiate and develop in the directions that make most sense in the life structure that her mate is constructing."[34] The woman's dream is simply not individualized as is the man's.

It is interesting to note that Steward discovered that women who chose the traditional route of marriage/motherhood oftentimes began to look for ways of being in the world that were more individualized as they become older. They were trying to develop an entirely new dream. They no longer were content to just support *his* dream or his vision of the future. These women were more interested now in developing their own inner selves.

Levinson contends that the dream must be broad enough to allow for adaptation, but also to present a somewhat consistent picture to the young person of what he or she is, in the process of becoming an adult. He is referring to a more individualistic type of dream, which would suggest that a relational dream would in some way be flawed. The dream would be considered flawed if it limits the process of exploration and growth in the subsequent decade.

Since a relational dream cannot undergo the process of exploration and survive as an individualistic dream can, this would indicate that the relational dream is probably flawed.

Even women who are trying to develop themselves in both work and love at the same time were having difficulties. Scarf points out that these women are trying to develop two differing kinds of selves simultaneously. "In her intimate life, as she relates to her opposite sex partner, this young woman is expected to be someone warm and emotional, nurturant, expressive, non-competitive, supportive, more compliant, and so forth. (Otherwise, she's 'castrating,' or, worse yet, 'unfeminine.') The built-in conflict, however, and the ambivalent sets of signals with which she must deal, stem from the fact that in her occupational world she'll have to show much more of the typically masculine forms of behavior—self-assertion, competitiveness, control, dominance, a push toward mastery (including mastery over men). The ambitious woman seems to be required, both by inward and outward pressures, to evolve not a single 'self' or personality, but two at once."[35]

Scarf is not surprised that many women consequently finally choose to disconnect themselves from one or the other of these role options. For they believe that it is probably better to return to the career race later on, when other life issues have been settled.

For men, though, the sexual and occupational role behaviors are far more synonymous. Scarf mentions that in both working and loving, men are expected to be more assertive, aggressive, masterful, etc. Men do not experience this same ambivalence or this strain between two very different ways of being as women do.[36]

Levinson's second task—that of forming a mentor relationship—is equally problematic as shown in our discussion above. The third and fourth tasks, forming an occupation and forming love relationships, marriage and family, are exceedingly difficult for a woman to accomplish simultaneously. As we have seen, many women feel it comes down to an "either/or" choice.

The problem of differing societal expectations for men and women is a serious one—more so for women. Kirsten Amundsen very aptly illuminates this special female problem. "So powerful is the ideology of sexism, so ubiquitous and clamorous its doctrine, that despite all evidence to the contrary women themselves have been trapped in it. No greater tribute could be made to its persuasiveness than the continued insistence on the part of many women that all they want in life is wifely happiness and maternal fulfillment. The contrast in horizons and ambitions between women and men is here immediate and striking. What would we think, after all, of a man who professed such limited goals? For men it is human fulfillment that is to be sought—not just satisfaction in marriage and fatherhood. But, then, men are *persons,* individuals with needs and interests and drives that transcend their sex roles. Women, it would seem, do not quite make it into that exalted category—or so sexist ideology would have it."[37]

The young woman has had a number of obstacles placed in her way and has made only limited progress with the tasks of the novice phase. Nevertheless, the years are slipping by and it is time for her at the age of about twenty-eight to begin the transition into the "summer" of her life and to begin working on the additional tasks posed by this particular season.

The Summer of a Woman's Life
(Age 28–39)

The long, dry summer follows the spring. This is the season of profound questioning. All the researchers on the subject of life-stages agree that this is a crisis time for adults. Assurance wavers, life begins to look more difficult and painful, and self-reflection churns up new questions: What is life all about? Why can't I be accepted for what I am, and not what others expect me to be?

The summer of a woman's life can be said to consist of an "Age Thirty Transition" period (age 28–32), and a "Settling Down" period (age 32–39). I believe that this transition period is one of the most difficult stages a woman must face. How a woman deals with this crisis will markedly influence the remainder of her life.

The Age Thirty Transition (Age 28–32)

The Age Thirty Transition frequently begins with a vague uneasiness, a feeling that something is missing or wrong in one's life, and that some change is needed if the future is to be worthwhile. An adult must ask questions dealing with the life one has created. What parts must I give up or appreciably change? What is missing from my life? Toward the end of the Age Thirty Transition the woman's orientation should be more toward the future. She should have found a new life direction and made new choices, or strengthened her commitment to choices already made.[38]

The Age Thirty Transition is an opportunity for the woman to work on the flaws and limitations of the Early Adult Structure and to create the bases for a new, more satisfactory structure with which to start settling down. There is a period of four to five years in which to question and reappraise the earlier structure and to ask: What have I done with my life? What do I want to make of it? What new directions shall I choose?

Wendy Steward's analysis of her data on women confirmed that the period of around age thirty is viewed as an opportunity for women to make desired changes in their twenties' life structure. "The quality of this new life structure appeared dependent, to a large extent, on the quality of the life structure formed during the twenties." Of particular interest to Steward were the consequences of a woman having created a life structure based on marriage and family versus having remained single during her twenties. The data suggested that "where serious flaws in the twenties' life structure are not addressed around age thirty, these flaws might emerge disruptively during subsequent periods of development and limit the process of further psychosocial growth."[39]

We can get a sense of the desperation women are feeling during this transition in the following quotes. Barbara

Marx Hubbard, eleven days after her marriage, has the following thoughts:

> Wrapped in bright, red paper with a big, yellow bow, I'm married, in a room with my husband. . . . Every once in a while I realize that my life is at stake—my own growing, exciting, creative life. I'm sick to death of floundering about. I'm not in competition with Earl, but his creativeness is a constant reminder of my own death. His talent and fluency tighten up my own rather sticky abilities. I need warmth to make them melt. His heat is hotter than mine and so holds me in. Or perhaps I need the cold to make me feel my own warmth to regain confidence. Without that, the best of abilities retire, much less my lukewarm genius. I can't afford to let it slip away any longer. If I write every night, it helps.[40]

Another woman at age twenty-five:

> I've done everything women are supposed to do—gardening, hobbies, antiques, social teas with the neighbors, work for the hospital guild and participating in the local P.T.A. I can do it all, and to a point I enjoy it, but I still feel empty, with a big sense of nothing, when it is all over. I love my husband, I was never cut out to be a career woman, and I love my children, but inside I am discontented and desperate. I feel I have no personality, there is no me—Who am I?[41]

A suburban housewife reflects on her life:

> I think, after the age of thirty I was grown up, and whatever I did now was on my own. You don't go for help after thirty, you do it—you have to do it your-

> self. . . . I had the feeling: If I were ever left alone,
> would I be able to cope with myself? . . . I also had the
> feeling: Was I content with everything I had? I remem-
> ber sitting watching the soap operas—my kids would be
> taking their naps, my house would be spic and span . . .
> all of a sudden I wasn't content. I wanted to go places. I
> was bored—sick and tired of staying home watching
> their "world turn" and mine wasn't![42]

These thoughts give us a sense of the crisis involved at this time. It is interesting that all of the women in Steward's sample, when approaching age thirty, either abandoned the twenties' life structure, or attempted to break away from it, or seemed confused about how to build on it.[43]

It is of paramount importance to realize that changes can be made now. If "the dream" of the twenties only reflected the woman's attempt to comply with or defy her parents, or if an overly restrictive dream leads to a premature restriction of exploration during the twenties, the period around age thirty must be used to make dramatic changes both in the dream and in the resulting life structure.[44]

This is an imperative because, as Steward's data suggests, where serious flaws are then present in the life structure but not acknowledged, these flaws might emerge disruptively during subsequent periods of development, or at least limit the process of further psychosocial growth until they are adequately addressed.[45]

Steward's research also indicates that some women might undergo an extended age thirty crisis. The normal transition takes about four years but for some it could take as long as eight years. This is a striking contrast to Levinson's study of men whose transitions were typically four years.

Steward states that some women, having dismantled the major elements of their twenties' life structure, were exhibiting significant difficulties in terminating the reassessment stage and forming a new life structure in their early to mid-thirties. Her data suggests that this was because these women had made a particularly bad start in forming a provisional life structure during their twenties, and it was not surprising to Steward that in their efforts to improve their lives, they were running into substantial internal and external hurdles.[46]

Her research results also indicate that when a woman pursued a career and/or remained single during her twenties, a move toward a more integrated and stable life structure takes place around thirty, as Levinson also concluded. But for the women who made early commitments to marriage and motherhood, her data suggests that a new life structure may be formed in the thirties with some of the exploratory quality that Levinson attributes to the twenties' life structure. This exploration can be very problematic for some women because they may have to make an agonizing choice between continued stability and further personal growth.[47]

Levinson contends that the order of his developmental periods is fixed, and that one cannot successfully accomplish the tasks of one period without having adequately dealt with the tasks of earlier periods. But Steward's research proves that this was not necessarily the case for all women.

Another special problem for women that arises at this time relates to the establishment of a home and family life by their early thirties. Steward states that her data supported "the conception of the period around age thirty as a time when women feel increased urgency to establish a satisfactory home life if this task has not been accomplished during the twenties. When a woman has, in addition, a strong commitment to building a career, the data supported the need for integration of these potentially conflicting components into the life structure beginning at this time."[48]

While Levinson discusses the importance for bachelors of coming to terms with the issue of marriage during the Age Thirty Transition, there is no evidence that marriage for a man around age thirty results in the dramatic reordering of priorities of the life structure as would seem to be the case for women. Steward believes that for women who have not married or had children by their late twenties, an increased sense of urgency to do so is experienced around age thirty.[49]

The Age Thirty Transition is also often accompanied by an increase in marital dissatisfaction. Steward associates this with a need in women to become less dependent on their husbands and to form a more egalitarian relationship with them.

It is my opinion that women have a difficult time meeting this need because egalitarian relationships appear to be rare. I think this is due to the fact that there are many men who are threatened by independent, assertive women. These men wish to relate to dependent, emotionally needy women because they lack a belief in themselves and fear women who work and think. They really dislike women and consequently worry about keeping the upper hand. They do not recognize that masculine strength has nothing to do with ruling or controlling. If a woman is in a relationship with this type of man, she jeopardizes her marriage if she attempts to form her own identity. And when a marital relationship is unable to accommodate reassessment during the Age Thirty Transition, a woman may have to choose between sacrificing either the stable family life or further personal growth. In Steward's study, women responded to this dilemma either by obtaining a divorce or by maintaining the marriage but emotionally withdrawing into extra-familial activities or liaisons.[50]

It is my own opinion that most women, if forced to make such a crucial choice, elect to stay in the marriage at the significant cost of ego autonomy. This is due to the woman's dependence on the male for support and security. After all, she is financially dependent on the husband; this is almost inevitable in contemporary marriage given the income and earnings inequality of men and women. The societal obstacles placed in the path of divorced women with children are tremendous. It is no wonder that women will stay in psychologically unhealthy marriages. The costs of obtaining ego autonomy appear to the woman to outweigh the benefits of obtaining it.

Lillian Rubin points out the dangers women face when they make moves to change their lives. For if the woman attempts to disengage from a "family first" orientation, she is threatening the very existence of the family to which she has devoted her life. For if she really means finally to take care of herself—to hear her own inner voice, to respond to its message—she must deal with the fear, also grounded in the reality of modern life, that her marriage will founder.[51]

Rubin goes on to mention that the possibility of divorce frightens women. They see friends go from rich to poor, from a life of relative comfort to one of deprivation, and the prospects that things will get much better financially are not good for most women who divorce after many years of marriage and financial dependency. For women who had lived in professional middle-class marriages, divorce meant going from $45,000 a year to $14,000; for those from working-class marriages, from $19,000 to $7,000.[52]

As Rubin states: "Such realities alone could account

for women's fear of divorce, for the fact that so often they give up their own needs at seemingly slight pressure from their husband. Indeed, these income figures alone could explain why women often seem so powerless to shape their own lives. If money talks, these figures shout. The message is clear: Be careful. Don't take on a fight you're not prepared to finish—one whose outcome you can't predict, whose loss could have life-shattering consequences."[53]

Also, one must remember that the older a woman gets the fewer chances for remarriage. The fears women have are real and put a great deal of pressure on women to maintain the status quo. The consequence of all this is that women don't readily find an answer to the question "What am I going to do with the rest of my life?" And for many women, they don't dare to look for one.

Rubin points out that women are faced with difficult problems that have no pat answers or simple solutions, and poses the question: "Who will suffer the risks to continue the search for self despite the anxieties it generates; despite the guilt, fear, and pain; despite the redoubtable obstacles the world continues to put in her way?" Rubin answers: "Perhaps only those who say: 'I take the risk because I have to.' Perhaps only those who feel: 'It's the only way.' Perhaps only those who believe: 'There's nothing less than my life at stake.' "[54]

The fear of divorce is not the only problem women are facing. Another problem is well expressed by Penelope Washbourn: "Marriage literally makes women sick as they try to cope with the complex demands of being housewife, valet, mistress, mother, and often outside wage earner. Women are doomed to incompetence and a feeling of failure in their attempt to juggle all these expected roles."[55]

Washbourn points out that the attempt to find a total identity in a concept of oneself as primarily wife and mother leads to destructive effects, not only on the development and growth of the personality of the woman, but also ultimately on the husband and children. "Until a woman goes beyond this form of dependency, there can be no real relationship, and she can experience no real sense of identity. She will behave as a vengeful influence on those around her. The negative role of bitch is almost built into a woman's role and it surfaces at the heart of the duality of marriage if this is the only place where she has a chance to exercise power."[54]

Washbourn further states:

> Finding the thread of her identity in and through the current structure of marriage is well-nigh impossible within the present patriarchal and sex-linked preconceptions of married roles. The romantic myth of the bride who gives herself totally to the man she loves, expecting the structure of being a wife to substitute for a continuing sense of responsibility for one's individuality, remains the most demonic form of the meaning of marriage for women.[57]

The harm done to children by a woman who seeks her whole identity through marriage and motherhood is illuminated by psychologist Irene Claremont de Castillejo:

> Life insists on being lived, and anything that belongs to life which is allowed to lie dormant has to be lived by someone else. If we do not accept our shadow we force our children to carry the burden of our undeveloped capacities. They may become mediocre scientists or artists because we denied our own talents. They may become doctors, which they are not suited to be, because we failed to use our innate capacity for healing, or inept politicians to fulfill our unlived ambitions.[58]

Another profound insight is provided by Peter Koesten-baum. He feels that mothers and fathers sometimes love their children in an inauthentic manner. They resist feeling this same degree of love for themselves, for, in reality, the child is really they and they are saying that this is how they wish they could be loved. He states:

> The child embodies the dreams of the parents. Thus, many parents—thank God!—are devoted deeply to their children. Furthermore, people who are otherwise quite sober, rational, just, and composed can become incredibly emotional and irrational—technically known as epileptoid apoplexy—when their commitment, love and hopes for their children are threatened. If we now invert that love for children, then in place of the child there stands you. The child for whom you have this profound love, these hopes, and this unqualified commitment and for whom you weep your tears is really you. That is what it means to take yourself seriously. To this we all aspire.[59]

Sociologist Nancy Chodorow in her book *The Reproduction of Mothering* points out the harm this type of mothering has on both child and mother:

> Those very capacities and needs which create women as mothers create potential contradictions in mothering. A mother's sense of continuity with her infant may shade into too much connection and not enough separateness. Empathy and primary identification, enabling anticipation of an infant's or child's needs, may become an unconscious labeling of what her child ought to need, or what she thinks it needs. The development of a sense of autonomous self becomes difficult for children and leads to a mother's loss of sense of self as well. That women turn to children to complete a relational

triangle, or to recreate a mother-child unity, means that mothering is invested with a mother's often conflictual, ambivalent, yet powerful need for her own mother. That women turn to children to fulfill emotional and even erotic desires unmet by men or other women means that a mother expects from infants what only another adult should be expected to give.[60]

Chodorow further comments that recent research suggests that children need consistency of care and the ability to relate to a small number of people stably over time. They do not require an exclusive relationship to one person. It is Chodorow's view that exclusive single parenting is bad for mother and child alike. She believes this because mothers in such a setting are liable to overinvest in and overwhelm the relationship. It is her contention that children are better off in situations where love and relationship are not a scarce resource controlled and manipulated by one person only.[61]

It can thus be argued that too much "mother smothering" can be just as damaging to a child as too little. This type of mother can have a destructive influence on a child. It is my opinion that many women who have sacrificed their own growth for their families have been both a cause and a casualty of their divorces. After all, nobody wants to spend life with someone who has no other choice, and children who have been raised by a mother who gave up her life for them almost always spend years on a therapist's couch learning to spit in her eye.

Perhaps such comments might encourage our woman to reassess the costs and benefits of making some crucial (and sometimes painful) choices in the Age Thirty Transition. The extent to which she is able to do so will ultimately determine the remaining seasons of her life. If the developmental tasks of the Age Thirty Transition have been accomplished our woman is now ready for Settling Down.

Settling Down—Becoming One's Own Woman (Age 32-39)

The underlying tasks of this period are to settle for a few key choices, to create a broader structure around them, to invest oneself as fully as possible in the various components of this structure, and to pursue long-range plans and goals within it. This involves (a) establishing one's niche in society, and (b) working at "making it."[62]

Steward's findings suggest that the age of the onset of "Settling Down" varies significantly among women. Some may achieve an integration of their life structure by age thirty-one to thirty-two, while others fail to do so by thirty-five.

It would appear that the term "Settling Down" may not adequately describe the complexities of this period for women. Steward points out that women who remain single in their twenties are now attempting to form the bases for a more stable life structure in the thirties within which more permanent commitments can be made, specifically regarding marriage and family.

In contrast, women who make commitments to marriage and family while in their twenties now begin to question their desire to continue this total commitment to the family. For these women the Age Thirty Transition forms the groundwork for a process of "opening up" in the thirties. This "opening up" process may actually involve the formation of an individualistic dream and/or the formation of a mentor relationship, and thus can incorporate developmental tasks which Levinson attributes to the earlier "Entering the Adult World" period (age 22–28).[63]

Barbara Estes' study of women in their thirties, like Wendy Steward's, is one of the few based on empirical data and sheds much light on the developmental process of the thirties.

Estes notes that some women begin in their thirties to resist what they have seen as society's rules, realizing that they want something different and feeling they are entitled to it. Having discovered from her research some of the same findings as Steward's, she states:

> The beginning of this reworking of identity is often a sense of dissatisfaction, sometimes mild: "I'm trying to say, What have I done? Suddenly your children don't need you as much as they did. . . . While I enjoyed the freedom of having them in school, it wasn't enough. I thought 'Gee, what could I do?' It was desperation that sent me back to school. It was real depression. I felt like I was always waiting for my husband to come home and I didn't want to spend my life waiting for someone else."[64]

Estes believes that when a woman makes her own choices rather than acting on what she thinks is expected, there is a sense of being personally responsible. She also sees a process taking place in the thirties that she calls "expanding awareness of possibilities, picking up earlier threads, acceptance that not all alternatives are possible." This process sounds very similar to the tasks Levinson assigns to the Settling Down period.

Estes states that the women she interviewed for her study were at various stages of this process: "Some were becoming aware of new possibilities and wondering which ones to try; others had tried many new activities and settled on one that seemed to supply a purpose to their lives."[65]

For most women, time goes faster in the thirties than previously. Sometime in the thirties one comes to the awareness that one won't live forever, whereas previously there was plenty of time. One woman states: "After I passed thirty, I felt, you know, half your life is over and, if you're going to start anything, it probably would be a good idea to do it now. Not when you're forty."[66]

The awareness of the finiteness of one's life-span is frequently accompanied by depression or even panic: "The thing that felt really crazy a couple of months ago was feeling like I was done, that I'd realized a plateau and this was it in my life." Another woman describes the following: "My thirty-fifth birthday was just awful! I felt like I was getting old. I had never wanted to have children of my own, and then all of a sudden I realized perhaps I did and it probably wouldn't happen."[67]

Estes' work resulted in several other interesting findings:

1. All the women interviewed were reworking their identity in their thirties, the task Erikson assigns to adolescence. (This finding, that women's identity has not been achieved by the time of entering adulthood, is corroborated in the research of others.)

2. The women in this study support the findings of Neugarten in that they show increased emphasis in middle age (age thirty-five to forty-five) on self-utilization rather than the self-consciousness of youth. Neugarten's reworking of identity from *shoulds* to *what I want* is similar to Estes' description of the increased "interiority" of middle age.

3. All of the subjects experienced difficulty in focusing on both home and work (whether paying or volunteer

work), with a balance between the two achieved by only half of the women and then only in their thirties.[68]

Dr. Jean Baker Miller, a psychiatrist, in discussing women's task of "Becoming Oneself" that occurs in the thirties, mentions:

> In our time we have heard a great deal about people's lack of authenticity. What we cannot hear so clearly is that, for half the population, the attempt at authenticity requires a clear and direct risk. For women to act and react out of their own being is to fly in the face of their appointed definition and their prescribed way of living.[69]

She believes that each woman has to risk focusing on her own desires and needs, even if it means displeasing others. Often the important other is the person in whom her major emotional attachment is invested. And if it is the male partner, her whole economic livelihood and social status are usually involved as well.

Miller strongly believes that the woman in her thirties *must* take some crucial risks if she wishes to grow into an authentic individual. The woman must realize that authenticity and subordination are totally incompatible. She talks about this need to take risks:

> As soon as many women think of incurring someone else's displeasure—especially a man's—they equate it with abandonment. The risk, in its psychic meaning and impact, becomes the risk of abandonment and condemnation. (The woman will be left, because *she* was wrong and bad.) But whether the man would, in fact, leave or not, women are conditioned to feel he will. For women this is often one of the greatest and most frightening risks. In some cases the man does not, in fact,

leave as the woman pursues her course; in others, the woman herself leaves and perhaps finds better relationships altogether. But the crucial factor is that she must take the initial risk—as a psychological step. If women avoid taking this risk, in most cases they cannot begin the journey. It is only when the woman can move away from thinking of first pleasing another and conforming to his desires and expectations that she can even begin to know herself. With the economic and psychological realities today, this risk is still huge.[70]

It is my own opinion that for most women this risk is assessed as being too great. As I go about my own business of living, I see suburbia filled with these women who refuse to take the risk. But I don't want to blame them because I believe that when an individual feels powerless a total feeling of impotence is the ultimate result.

Dr. Smith believes that the woman's problem lies in the usual goal of securing the realtionship *first*, before the woman truly knows herself. She points out that this happens because male–female relationships have been so effectively structured by society to deflect women away from their own reactions and fulfillment.[71]

It is certainly true that women do encounter a great number of obstacles in the summer of their lives. While the sociologist in me wants to blame a sexist society for the woman's seemingly insurmountable problems, the philosopher in me fears that by doing so I will rob the woman of the freedom and responsibility of taking charge of her own life. As Peter Koestenbaum states:

The solution to the problem of feminine roles must be primarily personal, rather than public and sociological. A woman must solve the issue as her own inner dilemma rather than as a matter for social criticism and social

action. . . . Since the problem of roles is her symbolization of the problem of meaning of life, it is the most
serious of all her problems, demanding an uncompro-
mising, immediate, and absolutely true solution.[72]

Koestenbaum also points out:

The fact of her free will shows that the solution to the
problem of feminine roles is exclusively the individual's responsibility. To blame others for the problem is
to run counter to the facts of human experience; it is to
run away from the problem, having made the decision
not to solve it. A woman freely chooses whether to
solve her problem or whether to ignore it, and if she
chooses to solve it, she also freely chooses the meth-
ods. . . . How she approaches her problem, how seriously she takes it, how much effort she expends on it, how
determined she is in carrying out her decision—these
choices are exclusively hers to make, and on the freely
chosen quality of these choices depend the success and
happiness of her life.[73]

While what Koestenbaum is saying is true, I do believe
that women's problems are tremendously exacerbated by
living in a sexist society. The woman oftentimes is miser-
able but she doesn't really understand why. It will only be
through education and "consciousness raising" that these
women will be able to visualize their options and thereby
be capable of utilizing their freedom in order to take responsibility for their lives. But there are women who use
living in a sexist society as an excuse for leading ineffective
lives. I believe this to be an invalid response and ultimately
counterproductive.

Our woman is growing older during the long summer,
and the fruit is slowly ripening with nothing much in the

woman herself to show for it. But now, at forty, the fruit is almost ripe. "Unsuspected fruit, fruit which has swelled and grown unheeded, is now ready and waiting to be plucked. The autumn of a woman's life is far richer than the spring if only she becomes aware in time and harvests the ripening fruit before it falls and rots and is trampled underfoot."[74]

If the woman has prepared for the autumn before the long, dry summer is over, her life will be meaningful and she'll be on her way to achieving ego autonomy. Let us continue our journey with our woman as she enters into the "autumn" of her life.

Autumn and *Winter*

The Autumn of a Woman's Life (Age 39–65)

The Mid-Life Transition (Age 39–45)

The autumn begins with another transition phase. This period begins around forty and typically lasts about five years.

The Mid-Life Transition is a bridge between early adulthood and middle adulthood. And as in all transitions, the woman must come to terms with the past and prepare for the future. The three major tasks of this transition period are:

1. To terminate the era of early adulthood. The woman needs to review her life in that era and evaluate what she has done with it.

2. To take her first steps toward the initiation of middle adulthood. Although she is not yet ready to start building a new life structure, she can begin to modify the negative elements of the present structure and to test new choices.

3. To deal with the polarities that are sources of deep division in her life. By doing so she will be undergoing the

process of individuation. Individuation is defined by Carl Jung as the developmental process through which a person becomes more uniquely individual. The term refers to the changes in a person's relationship to himself and to the external world. According to Levinson, the four polarities whose resolution is the principal task of mid-life individuation are (a) young-old, (b) destruction-creation, (c) masculine-feminine, and (d) attachment-separateness.[75]

The need to reappraise the past arises in part because of a heightened awareness of mortality. Every individual must come to terms with the issue of "death." The woman must reconsider the past out of a need to use the remaining time more wisely. There is the continual search for meaning in one's life.

It is now important to ask: What do I really get from and give to my husband, children, friends, work, community—and self? What is it I truly want for myself and others? What are my central values and how are they reflected in my life? What are my greatest talents and how am I using (or wasting) them? What have I done with my early dream and what do I want with it now? Can I live in a way that combines my current desires, values and talents? How satisfactory is my present life structure—how suitable for the self, how viable in the world—and how shall I change it to provide a better basis for the future?[76]

In reappraising one's life a person discovers how much of it has been based on illusions.[77] Consequently a strong sense of disillusionment sets in. The woman needs to come to an awareness that some of the long-held assumptions and beliefs about herself and her world are not valid. This becomes particularly relevant to the woman who has invested all of her energy into her children or spouse and realizes, when the children leave home, that the "meaning" of her life is also gone. This woman may especially need to make new choices by creating a new identity for herself and thereby returning meaning to her life.

It is now important for the woman to modify the earlier life structure by making some choices. She may make some drastic changes in her life, which may involve divorce, remarriage, career change, etc. Or the woman may make some less obvious changes in her marital relationship, family life, or career.

A primary task of this transition is to modify the life structure of the thirties and to create the basis for a new structure appropriate to middle adulthood. The final test of the success of the developmental work done at this stage is how satisfactory the life structure is which emerges from it. "Whatever the nature of the developmental work done, and however modest or profound the structural changes wrought, the individual's life in the mid-forties will differ in crucial respects from that in the late thirties."[78]

Undergoing the process of individuation is the last task of this transition period. (This process of individuation is almost identical to what we earlier named as the goal of personality development—ego autonomy. Thus ego autonomy and individuation can be used interchangeably as we continue the study of women's development.) Individuation should be going on throughout the life cycle. With the termination of an existing structure and the initiation of a new one, the woman is simultaneously undergoing the process of individuation. Therefore, the woman has several opportunities to work on this particular developmental process.[79]

Many investigators of middle-age emphasized certain characteristics of this developmental stage. Erikson gives primary emphasis to generativity vs. stagnation. Jaques believes that the central issue at mid-life is coming to terms with one's own mortality: "A man must learn now, more deeply than before, that his own death is inevitable and that he and others are capable of great destructiveness."[80] Jung states that a new effort at individuation begins at mid-life and continues through the remaining years.

Levinson has developed four polarities that must be confronted and reintegrated into a person's life. I will briefly describe each of these.

(1.) *Young-Old.* Being young and being old symbolize different things. The two must be integrated. "The symbolization of being both old and young—of death and rebirth, destructuring and restructuring, mortality and immortality—is inherent in the very nature of a developmental transition. We feel old in that a phase in our lives is coming to an end and must be permitted to pass. Yet we also feel young, since the potential for a new period carries with it the qualities of rejuvenation and growth."[81]

It is also within the polarity of Young/Old that a person must come to terms with death. Philosophers would certainly agree that confronting one's own death, and the resulting powerful wish for immortality, are a universal occurrence. This is one of the great issues of human existence.

Playwright Lillian Hellman, who wrote *Autumn Garden,* sums up this feeling:

> I suppose the point I had in mind is this—you come to a place in your life when what you've been is going to form what you will be. If you've invested yourself in life, you're pretty certain to get a return. If you are inwardly a serious person, in the middle years it will pay off.[82]

In the middle years it is hard to know how much one has wasted oneself or invested in life, and what kind of further return one will have during the middle years.[83] What we need, according to Maggie Scarf is an acceptance of our origins, and the life that we have had, including all the mourned and ultimately integrated pain and suffering that our one and only life cycle may have contained. We need to accept who we are and who we have become.[84]

2. *Destruction-Creation.* In recognizing one's own mortality one becomes more aware of destruction as a universal process. Knowing this, a person desires to become more creative—to generate life. "The acute sense of his own ultimate destruction intensifies a man's wish for creation. His growing wish to be creative is accompanied by a greater awareness of the destructive forces in nature, in human life generally, and in himself."[85]

It is coming to terms with evil that is involved here: the evil caused by nature ("Acts of God") and the even worse type of evil caused by man's/woman's inhumanity to man/woman. "To have the power to do great good, we must bear the burden of knowing that we will cause some harm—and in the end, perhaps, more harm than good."[86]

3. *Masculine-Feminine.* Each individual has both masculine and feminine qualities. Peter Koestenbaum explains this polarity:

> Each of us has a masculine potential—strong, individual, aggressive, independent, leading, hard—and a feminine component—trusting, accepting, loving, compassionate, caring, mothering, passive, nurturing. . . . Each person has the opportunity to develop his or her potential for leading as well as accepting.[87]

The authentic person is one who can express both masculine and feminine qualities and balance them successfully.

4. *Attachment-Separateness.* Levinson explains that to be attached is to be engaged, involved, needy, plugged in,

seeking, and rooted. At the opposite end of the pole is separateness. This is not the same thing as isolation or aloneness. "A person who is alone, yet actively involved in planning a future activity or in feeling resentful over a past rejection, is nonetheless firmly attached to the external world."[88] Separateness fosters individual growth and creative adaptation, but it can be harmful when carried to extremes. "A person is separate when he is primarily involved in his inner world—a world of imagination, fantasy, and play."[89]

Persons of all ages and occupations must deal with the Attachment-Separation polarity. "If we become too separate, our contact with the world is lost and our capacity for survival jeopardized. If we become too attached to the environment, we endanger our capacity for self-renewal, growth and creative effort."[90]

Attachment bonds have been very useful and extremely essential to our species' survival and development. Consequently we resist with great biological force any disruption of attachments. Maggie Scarf points out that this fact is even more true for the female because she is more "people oriented" from the moment she is born. A female tends to value herself and gains esteem from her loving attachments. Scarf states:

> The outer membrane of the female's psyche is, somehow, more permeable; it is not distinct and delimited from the psyches with which she is emotionally enmeshed. (Males, in contrast, tend to keep "my own self" and others far more clearly separate; and to have greater conflicts about intimacy, i.e., permitting the other in.) But because, in the case of the woman, the context has often been incorporated into the inner being, the loss or threatened loss of a powerful attachment can be experienced as a devastation of the

person's own ego, her own self. The loss of that bond
feels like death itself because the person's entire being
has been defined in relation to it. She is then faced
with the terrifying question of who she is, and what she
is, without it. She is faced with the prospect of living
on her own (in terms of giving up dependence on that
relationship to tell her who she is and supply her reasons for being). This is, in my view, where the true vulnerability lies: for "aloneness" of this sort is something
for which many women are unprepared. So unprepared,
in fact, that a woman is often readier to experience as
guilt, anger, and reproaches directed against the self,
what is, in fact, deep dismay and disappointment about
a close relationship.[91]

Consequently, it is more problematic for the woman to integrate both attachment and separateness within her personality.

It is also important to note that the Mid-Life Transition
requires a woman to reduce her heavy involvement in the
external world. In order to do the work of reappraisal and
de-illusionment, she must turn inward. Thus the major developmental task of middle adulthood is to find a better
balance between the needs of the self and the needs of society.

Our woman must confront the great polarities that create basic divisions between the individual and society. No
one can ever entirely overcome the divisions but each must
find new ways of being young/old, masculine/feminine,
destructive/creative, and attached/separate. There may be
much tension involved in balancing these polarities, but
this tension is what makes us feel truly alive and growing.

Some women have not come to terms with their individuality or their aloneness during earlier transition periods. They have not accomplished the necessary earlier tasks

and consequently they lack the inner and outer resources for creating an even minimally adequate life structure in middle adulthood. Some women are able to form a reasonably viable life structure. They perform specific roles for themselves and others—oftentimes only in a relational capacity—but their lives are lacking inner excitement and a sense of fulfillment. It is as if something were missing but they can't put their finger on just what it is.[92]

Some women are able to make a start in their Mid-Life Transition toward a middle adulthood that will have both satisfactions as well as burdens to be overcome. These women may find that middle adulthood is the most loving and creative season in the life cycle.[93]

But this is not the woman's last chance to work out these developmental tasks. These tasks can continue to be worked on throughout her life. Levinson states that around forty-five the individual runs out of energy to reappraise the past and reintegrate the polarities and it is time for a new period to set in—Middle Adulthood.[94]

Middle Adulthood (Age 45–50)

The main tasks of Middle Adulthood are to make crucial choices, give the choices meaning and commitment, and build a life structure around them.[95]

Levinson notes that some of the men in his study were able to make satisfactory provisional choices during their Mid-Life Transition. But in most cases the men were not able to form a stable structure by forty-five. The man needs more time to establish the choices in which a new life structure may be built. It may take him the rest of his life to accomplish this task. Levinson states: "In short, an integrated structure may emerge late or early in Middle Adulthood, or not at all. A man stays in this period, however, as long as his predominant developmental task is to create a satisfactory structure. The period ends when the task changes and he enters a new transition."[96]

This appears to be the same for women. We have all met women who at fifty years of age have not resolved the identity crisis of adolescence. It is my contention that very few women are able to resolve this crisis by the end of the seventeen to twenty-two-year-old transition period. Some women handle this task during the Age Thirty Transition, and some women never resolve it. I think that society is structured in such a way as to give women few opportunities to resolve their crisis of individuality. It may be that some men never resolve their identity crisis either, but their masculine identity rests on their successfully doing so while the woman's femininity rests almost solely on her relational capacities. Of course, the man may have problems with other developmental tasks that are easier for the woman. But the task of developing a sense of individuality is such a prerequisite for achieving ego autonomy that the woman may well go through life crippled by her inability to resolve the meaning of her personhood.

Supporting the theory that women generally come into mid-life with a flawed sense of identity, which often results in an intense feeling of anxiety, is the high incidence of depression in middle-aged women. Anywhere from two to five times as many women as men are likely to be depressed in this age group. Depression is a symptom that something is very wrong in a person's life, and is often a symptom of meaninglessness. The statistical evidence is clear and overwhelming: females from adolescence onward—and throughout every phase of the life cycle—are far more vulnerable to depression than are males.

I do not believe that it is just a problem of incorrect psychiatric labeling. Some researchers have claimed that the male-dominated mental health establishment labels women as depressed as a means of punishing women who do not adjust to and accept their "femininity" under the terms laid down by a male-dominated society. The woman who fails to accept her female role, along with the attendant inferior social status, isn't "behaving," and she gets labeled with a psychiatric diagnosis. Scarf believes that this diagnosis is a handy "medical" and scientifically respectable device for keeping women in their place.[97]

While I believe this may be true to a certain extent, I feel that there are just too many women psychologists who report seeing many women who are truly and very acutely in pain. Psychologist Phyllis Chesler states: "The women whom I have come to know well or only slightly, whom I've talked to at length or just a little, whom I've seen just once or several times over periods of months—were all suffering. They were in pain, and in need of help; there just was no question about it."[98]

Marcia Guttentag directed a nationwide study of what many consider to be an "epidemic" of depression among women. The Guttentag study concluded after analyzing the mental health statistics that there is much more depression among women. This fact may be very discomforting but it is real. "Not only was there the excess of treated depressions; moreover, there also seemed to be vast numbers of women who were depressed for various reasons, and who had many of the clear-cut symptoms of depression, but who were walking around, not realizing they 'had' anything, and therefore not seeking treatment."[99]

I am not at all surprised that women become depressed. I agree with Rubin that depression is an end result when clothes, furniture, entertainment, etc. that mean so much to the woman are not just pleasures, but are needs—needs born of an ill-formed sense of self, of the fear that deep inside there's nothing but emptiness. In order to avoid dealing with the fears of that inner void—with the terror that there is really nothing of substance on the inside—women turn to fixing up the outside. "Women struggle endlessly to fix their faces, their bodies, their homes. All to no avail. For the problem they're trying to alleviate, the pain they're trying to compensate, lies inside, not outside. And no amount of patching on the outside will give anything but a brief respite, temporary surcease from the restless strivings that drive them."[100]

What these women really need, according to Rubin, is to be engaged in activities and commitments that will still the fears and fulfill the yearnings—activities that foster the development of a strong inner sense of self, commitments that facilitate the belief that there is a solid core inside with an identity that is bounded and an integrity that is firm.[101]

Rubin points out that the pressures are harsh on a woman who dares not just to want something for herself but to reach out and take it—pressures both internal and external, pressures from a psychology and a society that long ago came together to keep her in her place. Thus, she suffers from guilt and anxiety over the course she has set and the consequences to her family. In far too many cases the ultimate result of this process is depression.[102]

Scarf tells us that there are some more optimistic theories that conclude that men and women are equally depressed but women are just more likely to go to a doctor for treatment. Women may be simply assuming the culturally "available" sick-and-dependent role when they are depressed, while men fail to seek medical attention. These researchers have claimed that the exorbitant number of depressed women could be a statistical red herring: men and women might be equally depressed, but men may not be counted as "cases" because they have never gone for treatment.[103]

But other researches state that this simply isn't the case. "For powerful evidence from so-called community studies indicates that women really are more depressed than men—irrespective of who does or who doesn't go to the doctor."[104] Scarf mentions one such community study that was done by Myrna M. Weissman, director of the Yale Depression Unit and an epidemiologist by training. Weissman's survey, like most others that have been done on this subject, has uncovered the same phenomenon: an almost frightening amount of depression among women respondents. And Weissman reports a steady rise in female depressions in the past decade. Her own research on suicide attempts among females indicates a similar trend. She states: "This has been well documented in several countries over the past ten years. And while all suicide attempters may not be depressed, I would say that most of them are."[105]

The big question is: Why? The possible answer of "female hormones" does not seem correct. "Endocrines may affect mood, in various ways and at particular times, but they don't really provide reasons for the huge differential in overall male and female rates of depressive illness."[106]

One explanation may have to do with the female trait of dependency. This trait seems to have a very pervasive and significant effect. Psychologist Judith Bardwick has summed this up well:

> The dependency, passivity, tears, and affection-seeking normal to both sexes in younger children are defined as feminine in older children, and girls can remain dependent and infantile longer. . . . Unless something intervenes, the girl will continue to have throughout

womanhood a great need for approval from others. Her behavior will be guided by the fear of rejection or loss of love. An independent sense of self-esteem can only evolve when the individual, alone, sets out to attain goals and, with reasonable frequency, achieves them.[107]

Maggie Scarf reports that her research on depression in women shows that women are differentially intrigued by the topics of separation and loss because they know that these are the areas of their greatest vulnerability and highest risk. Scarf points out that women tend to develop depressive symptoms in the "rupture of a powerful attachment" context far more than they do for any other.[108]

Scarf is not optimistic about a reduction in depression in women in the future. "Most women will, at some point in their lives, have to live alone; and most women will have to learn that they can, even in the absence of a strong emotional bond. They are going to have to learn to survive 'aloneness' in the same way that men sometimes have to learn they can, even in the wake of a failure. But such learning tasks are, I fear, not going to be easy ones. Depression among women, given the social climate that we inhabit, is not by any means going to disappear, to diminish: it is probably going to afflict women—as the uncertainty of their attachments increases—in greater and greater numbers. We are not about to eradicate depressive illnesses from our midst. The best that can be done is to survive them."[109]

The overall point is that women "receive ferocious training in a direction that leads away from thinking 'What do I want?' and toward 'What do they want or need of me?' " Self-esteem becomes dependent upon the esteem of those around one. Feelings of emotional well-being, a sense of one's own worthfulness as a person, "are hostages to the moods, attitudes, and approval of others."[110]

The depressed woman is someone who has lost. She

has lost "something" upon which she vitally depended. The "loss" in question is usually a loss of a crucially important and often self-defining emotional relationship. Her husband or children have left her. Her life crumbles and falls apart. The meaning has gone out of her life.

Men do not get depressed with such regularity over the rupture or threatened rupture of emotional bonds. Men get depressed over work issues, status, and success problems— difficulties in "making it" in the world at large. "Women may be upset by these same issues but they don't touch upon the same tender, raw nerve-ending of concern."[111]

If a woman rates herself in terms of the health of her emotional attachments, much more—a far greater amount of "self"—will be at risk in her loving connections. The woman will never be an individual and never even come close to living an authentic life. It is as if her sex had condemned her.

Claudeen Cline-Naffziger, in her article "Women's Lives and Frustration, Oppression, and Anger," states that when women can no longer regard themselves as individuals, cannot take action on their own, and can only consider themselves in terms of the man with whom they live, they are being oppressed by their socialization.

Cline-Naffziger believes that women are short-changed by counselors and therapists. Many counselors classify housewives as either schizophrenics or chronic depressives without considering the situation which produces the environmental stress. Although schizophrenia can rightly be called a "woman's disease," the responsibility of creating the schizophrenic lies more with our social structure than with the woman. "Why wouldn't the woman without skills, lacking sufficient education and possessing little power, perceive the world as an emergency situation? Why wouldn't she be depressed when her mate ignores her? This is not necessarily a regressive response on the part of an immature woman but rather a response based on reality when one has no other alternatives."[112]

Cline-Naffziger points out that angry women frequently seek help from counselors and psychologists. These helpers need to recognize the reality and justification for women's anger. Many women are taught that anger is not good and that it is not feminine. Women must be made aware of this myth about anger; they must be taught that anger is a common human emotion that needs to be acted upon. If it is completely repressed or subverted it can become evil. Anger itself is human. Anger indicates that action is needed.[113]

Peter Koestenbaum also reflects on the positive effects of anger when it is used authentically (as a precursor to change):

> Anger is one of the most important and effective coping devices against anxiety, for anger is protest, and protest is proof that the indomitable spirit of man has not been squelched. Indifference is the absence of a core, the experience of being an empty shell. Indifference is an empirical ego which is hollow; it is only an envelope. Anger, however, is the experience of the archetypal decision to be an ego, a self, a core, an identity. Anger is the last vestige of self-affirmation. If a child grows into an indifferent adult, he will have been defeated. But if he grows instead into an angry adult, he will maintain the posture of protest. His anger is his self-affirmation.[114]

Cline-Naffziger tells us that the best places to discover angry women are in the usual stereotyped positions:

> . . . housewives who manipulate husbands and children in order to achieve some vicarious life, secretaries

whose system of cross-filing is so complex that only they can trace the documents, teachers who hit pupils with rulers or inflict verbal abuse, and, last but not least, lovers in bed who are passive and non-participatory. Most depressed, bored, self-destructive, and dependent women are angry. They are depressed about the nature of their lives and bored with the limits set on their existence by their training, their society and their counselors. They are dependent after being brainwashed into knowing that their role is to satisfy men. They are self-destructive since it's not good to repress anger, and therefore it must turn inward and be used to deenergize. Angry women have lost the ability to fantasize. They are unable to share their dreams because they have given up dreaming. Angry women refuse to accept the responsibility for their own lives, since they have had so little opportunity to practice "response-ability."[115]

Barbara Estes has some suggestions on how counselors can help women in mid-life who are undergoing a crisis. She states that the mid-life crisis, when one realizes that life is not infinite, can be a gradual process, but for many it is a time of depression and even panic. If the counselor views this crisis as a normal developmental phase that can be resolved and is indeed an opportunity for increased growth, the woman can be reassured and use her energy for increased personal awareness, wise life-choices, and empathy with others, rather than denying the crisis with frantic activity, alcohol, or other potentially harmful defenses.[116]

It is my belief that dispensing medication freely (in the form of tranquilizers or other such drugs) is not helpful for these women. It simply masks the problem that needs to be dealt with. Also, the prevalent belief that the woman's depression may be caused by menopause is too simple an answer. Giving a woman medication to supply hormones will not bring meaning back into her life. She needs to be given avenues to explore her potential in order to expand her life. New horizons could be opened up for her, but she'll never take the opportunity to find this out if she is tranquilized into a continuous state of apathy.

Penelope Washbourn states:

> Menopause is a particularly deep crisis for women who have devoted themselves exclusively to mothering. The children are often grown up and leaving home as the woman wonders who she is now that her role as mother seems to be over. The demands of parenthood are over; the house is quiet, and the woman asks herself, Is there anything left? The end of her role of mother carries no accolades, no promotion, no thanks. The children are often grateful to be gone after the confrontation of the adolescent years. The woman who has found her identity exclusively in mothering faces the crisis of middle life with the least resources. . . . She feels tricked and cheated and that her children are ungrateful. She experiences no joy that the demands of parenthood are over, but emptiness. The promise given her that she will find herself through motherhood has proven hollow. She is no longer "needed," no longer loved; she feels no productive role in society.[117]

Washbourn goes on to point out the paradox that the woman's attempt to live up to the traditional image of mother or wife who gives her life for her children means that she, above all, has neglected her own personal and spiritual development. For such a woman, this is the hardest challenge. "The ability to recognize the nature of this crisis, to express the fears, confusion, regrets, and bitterness, will allow the woman to come into a new life as the process of mourning for the end of youth gives way to the re-emergence of hope."[118]

Some researchers are more optimistic about the mid-life crisis in women. Florine B. Livson did a study of middle-aged women at the Institute of Human Development, University of California, Berkeley. She found that for a number of women the departure of children—once the process of separation is completed—often led to improved satisfaction in the post-parental years. Livson discovered that role changes in the middle years allow some women not only to adapt but also to expand their psychological horizons. Parts of the personality that were suppressed because they were not congruent with the roles of mother and young adult may now surface to add new dimensions to the person.[119]

Consequently, it is very possible for a woman at the end of middle-age to be well on the road to ego autonomy. But I believe that this only happens if the woman is flexible enough to allow herself the chance to explore her potential to the fullest. Any woman who becomes locked into particular roles, who is not given the opportunity to broaden her horizons, or who does not realize that the opportunity is within her grasp, can come out of mid-life a tragically handicapped individual with greatly reduced chances of an authentic life.

Late Middle Adulthood (Age 50–65)

As the woman leaves her forties and begins her fifties, she enters into the Age Fifty Transition. The woman can now continue to work on the tasks of the Mid-Life Transition and can modify the life structure of the forties (Middle Adulthood). It can be another crisis for women who developed insufficiently in their Mid-Life Transition and then built an unsatisfactory life structure. It is Levinson's opinion that it is not possible to get through Middle Adulthood without having at least a moderate crisis in either the Mid-Life Transition or the Age Fifty Transition.[120]

Many women fear late middle adulthood for a number of reasons. For in fairy tales when the princess marries her prince, the story ends. We are told that the princess lived happily ever after. The curtain is pulled and that last long age of her life is concealed forever.[121]

Juanita Williams discusses how middle-aged women appear in fairy tales as wicked stepmothers or witches, almost never normal, mature women. "Ugly to the point of deformity, their personalities are distorted by jealousy and hatred. They have a penchant for cruelty, especially toward young girls, as in 'Cinderella' and 'Sleeping Beauty.' If fairy tales, like myths, are made in the deeper layers of the mind, out of the oldest fears and ruminative concerns of humans, then in them we see the reflections of feelings of fear and dread toward aging and toward the woman who is no longer young."[122]

It is Williams' opinion that women especially have good reason to fear the passing of youth. For her most socially valued qualities, her ability to provide sex and attractive companionship, and to have and nurture children, are expressed in the context of youth. In youth women are endowed with physical beauty and fertility. As a woman ages, she becomes less physically attractive and desirable, and her reproductive and nurturant functions are no longer relevant.[123]

Williams further points out that traditionally women have not been encouraged to develop those qualities which often improve with age, such as intellectual competence and the ability to apply mature wisdom to the solution of problems. Thus it is hardly surprising that depression and feelings of uselessness are identified so frequently in the literature on women who are over the age of fifty.[124]

In addition, according to Williams, "the problems that women express as they age seem to have a common motif of loss—loss of children, perhaps husband, loss of youth and physical attractiveness, loss of the regular reminder of femininity in the menopause, loss of purpose in life. The extent to which these changes are problems, however, depends upon cultural definitions and prescriptions for women and their roles, and upon idiosyncratic variables of personality and circumstances. No biological imperative programs women to feel worn out, useless, and depressed during the second half of life."[125]

Irene Claremont de Castillejo believes that the phrase "change of life" fits the situation that the fifty-year-old woman is now facing. She believes that menopause does not spell the end of life but simply a change of direction. With this "change of life" comes an enormous release of energy for some new venture in a new direction.[126]

The direction in which this energy flows can be positive. Some women develop latent talents such as painting, writing, or music. Other women start new careers or develop new goals and interests. De Castillejo points out that "there are also inumerable other women who can find no outlet. They suffer deeply, for energy which finds no channel in which to flow seeps into the ground and makes a marsh where nothing can be planted, where only slime and insects breed."[127]

De Castillejo describes what happens to these particular women: "Women who find they are no longer vitally needed by their families, yet have no other place where they can give themselves, sink into lassitude and finally fall ill. The magnates who organize society have hardly begun to notice this happening. The autumnal energy of countless older women escapes silently down the kitchen sink along with their tears."[128]

It is my belief that late middle adulthood is a particularly challenging time for women today. Today's woman is in limbo; she is in transition. The models for womanhood presented by her mother and grandmother are no longer useful. She now has to fumble through and make her own path by way of trial and error. This is another time of profound questioning.

Maggie Scarf very aptly describes this period of life: "The individual, male or female, will now move through a period of life in which the direction is downward, descending. It is, for both sexes, a time of estimating what have been one's profits, and what have been one's losses; a time of looking backward toward what has been and forward toward the shrinking future . . . of estimating what hopes, if any, still may possibly be realized. This is a period of living which, for obvious reasons, can become exquisitely painful."[129]

In addition, many women suffer a narcissistic injury at this age due to the changes in body image that are part of the aging process. The loss of youthful looks is seen by the woman as like the loss of an important relationship. Scarf points out that "the woman is filled with a sense of emptiness and grief, as though abandoned by her beloved. It may be, however, that what she is pining for, during this complex phase of living, is none other than the youthful, sexually appealing person that she used to be."[130]

According to Scarf, some women believe that a slightly sagging chin is Fate serving notice and that the remaining part of their lives will be spent in an ungratifying and unsatisfying situation which they will be powerless to alter. These women will face losing the only power they ever perceived themselves as owning—the power that goes along with being an alluring and attractive woman. Scarf believes that these women are far less assailed by the decline of hormones than by the decline of hope.[131]

In a more optimistic vein, there is some good news for women in middle age. Women who have faced earlier crises and worked successfully through them will find late middle age a positive experience. No woman may avoid through luck, or circumstances, or skill, or assistance, the tasks which each period imposes, although each may cope with the tasks differently. Attempts to escape the tasks central to any period of development and transition result in a blocking of growth and increase the severity of the crises which accompany subsequent transitions.

Optimism is expressed by Jan Cohen, Karen Coburn, and Joan Pearlman in their book *Hitting Our Stride.* They interviewed women who were single during their mid years and found that these particular women had grown a great deal. The authors state: "In circumstances many might not have chosen for themselves, they were not merely surviving, but prevailing, and, yes, often 'blooming.' Was it simply a matter of having no choice? That 'one does what one has to do'? Perhaps in part. Why, then, when men have been more prepared to function independently, when they have more financial security, more societal permission to pursue companions and sexual partners—why has research shown that women tend to fare better on their own? It may well be that the qualities we have been encouraged—and inclined—to develop, such as empathy, sensitivity, and adaptability, not only allow us to form close connections but give us a particularly strong sense of perspective and experience that stands us in good stead as women on our own in the middle years."[132]

It is my opinion that the qualities of empathy, sensitivity and adaptability are extremely valuable to women. What we as women need to do is to add to these the qualities of independence, potency, self-confidence and self-initiative. By doing so we would be well on our way to integration and wholeness and to living an authentic life.

How can we go about achieving this integration? Jean Baker Miller believes that to do so takes personal creativity. This type of creativity is a continuous process of bringing forth a changing vision of oneself, and of oneself in relation to the world. Out of this creation each person determines her/his next step and is motivated to take that next step. Miller states: "This vision must undergo repeated change and re-creation. Through childhood and adulthood, too, there are inevitable physical changes as one grows and then ages. These demand a change in one's relation to the world. Further, there are the continuous psychological changes that lead to more experience, more perceptions, more emotions, and more thought. It is necessary to integrate all these into a coherent and constantly enlarging conception of ones' life."[133]

Miller reminds us that each person repeatedly puts together a conceptualization that has never been put together before—that is, one constantly creates a personal vision. This vision is never exactly the same as anyone else's and it is never the same as the one we made yesterday. The more we are able to act in terms of our own conceptions, the more whole and authentic we feel. "Having acted, we can go back and 'correct' our conceptions about the world, about ourselves, about what we want."[134]

In order for a woman to create a personal vision for herself, she may need some additional support during this Age Fifty Transition. The woman may need help in realizing that she has many options that she may not have previously envisioned. A good counselor or therapist could be especially beneficial during this time. But Lillian Troll points out that a majority of psychotherapists believe that it is not worth it to treat anyone over the age of fifty. This is due to the fact that there is a persistent myth that the "over fifty" adult is tranquil, resistant to change, unresponsive to therapy, and destined to inevitable senility.[135]

Contradicting this theory that older people are resistant to change is a study done on the attitudinal changes in older adults. This study was designed to explore the potential for change in older age. The results showed that older women did not change their attitudes any less than young women. In fact, under normal conditions of presentation, they changed their attitudes more. This result contradicts the popular notion which suggests that older people are less able to change their attitudes than are younger people, and documents instead the potential for change in the older population.[136]

Thus change is indeed possible, and depression in menopausal and post-menopausal women could easily be eliminated. Scarf points out that the changes required of the woman are far more sweeping and more radical than they are for the man. "This phase of her life contains many more discontinuities, in terms of roles, functions, perceptions-of-self, than does the same phase in the life of the man. . . . One doesn't, for these reasons, actually need to resort to 'hormonal changes' as an explanation for the difficulties and real despair that some women experience during this perplexing state of female existence."[137]

Juanita Williams agrees with Maggie Scarf that women

become depressed during middle age because "they do not have enough *reasons* for satisfying action, and when they lose the one apparent reason upon which they predicated their lives—their femininity—their whole action world caves in." Williams believes that "menopausal depression is the consequence of confining women to a too narrow range of life choices or opportunities. It is a social and cultural phenomenon, for which the 'designers' of social roles are to blame. We create menopausal depression by not seeing to it that women are armed with more than one justification for their lives."[138]

Kenneth Israel also expresses concern over the plight of the woman over fifty. He sees her pulled in several directions and none of them are the sure path to salvation: "New forces create new demands and open new visions of action and roles, even though they may upset the applecart of established patterns. These new forces cause uncertainty and doubt about choices made long ago. The process of growing older leads naturally to a consideration of times past, often with regret, but sometimes with satisfaction. It also leads to disatisfaction when the sense of who one is and what one is worth has been based upon the reflected sparkle of the doings of others."[139]

Israel, a psychiatrist, has seen many older women who talk about their feelings of blank, yawning emptiness, of their deep doubts about how they can fill this void—or whether it is worth the effort. He believes that when marriage and children have been less than sustaining, the feelings of loss, disappointment, and depression are often too much. It is thus understandable to him why half the suicides in the United States are women over the age of forty-five.[140]

Levinson reports that after the Age Fifty Transition there is a more stable period devoted to the building of a second middle-adult structure. This is the age of fifty-five to sixty year period of life. If the woman is able to rejuvenate herself and enrich her life, the decade of the fifties can be a very fulfilling time.[141]

Around the age of sixty to sixty-five years is the transition period which Levinson has called the Late Adult Transition. The tasks of this transition are to conclude the efforts of middle adulthood and to prepare oneself for the "winter" of one's life. This is another period of hopefully significant development and represents a potentially major turning point in the woman's life. "To everything there is a season," and wisdom seems to come from adapting with "good enough grace" to the inevitable developmental tasks and seasons with which life, by its very nature, presents us.

Levinson reminds us:

> In every cross-era transition a new season is born and takes its initial shape. These transitions have a great effect on the future, but they never tell the whole story. Each new period makes its essential contribution to the life course. In every period we suffer because of the undone developmental work of previous periods—for ultimately these chickens do come home to roost—but we also have an opportunity to do further developmental work and to create a life more suitable to the self.[142]

As our woman reaches sixty-five years it is time for her "winter" to begin. If in the autumn of her life the woman has harvested the ripening fruit before it falls and rots, the winter which follows will not be barren.

Some modern conscious women do prepare for the autumn before the long, dry summer is over, but far too many women do not. These women feel that life is finished at fifty. Yet it is possible that latent possibilities may dance before our woman's unbelieving eyes in the winter of her life, and the winter for some women may then yield a fulfilled, self-actualized, authentic person.[143]

The Winter of a Woman's Life
(Age 65–?)

The winter which follows the autumn will not be barren if the harvest has been stored. For the woman who has accomplished the developmental tasks of the earlier periods, there will be a vital and meaningful winter season. She will have developed into a woman of true wisdom and personal nobility.

There does not appear to be an abundance of research done on personality development in late adulthood. Since Levinson's empirical data covered only through middle adulthood, he admits to be only speculating when discussing late adulthood. He does make some generalizations about this stage. One thing he mentions is that the character of living is now altered in fundamental ways as a result of numerous biological, psychological and social changes. Also, this era needs to be recognized as a very distinctive and fulfilling season in life.[144]

Levinson identifies the primary developmental task of late adulthood as that of finding a new balance between involvement with society and involvement with the self. The individual is experiencing more fully the process of dying, and should also have the possibility of choosing more freely one's mode of living. One can maintain the love of humanity, of one's own tribe, and of oneself, and still form a broader perspective and recognize more profoundly our human contradictions, creativity and destructiveness. Levinson states:

> Greater wisdom regarding the external world can be gained only through a stronger centering in the self. This does not mean that the individual becomes more selfish or vain. Just the opposite. It means that one becomes less interested in obtaining the rewards offered by society, and more interested in utilizing one's own inner resources. The voices within the self become, as it were, more audible and more worthy of one's attention. One continues to be actively engaged with the voices and realities of the external world, but one seeks a new balance in which the self has greater primacy.[145]

Erikson's final ego stage also occurs in this era. It begins around the age of sixty, and its key polarity is Integrity vs. Despair. In other words, one must achieve a kind of emotional closure. One must believe that her/his existence seems to have had order and meaning, rather than characterized by haphazardness and waste. Maggie Scarf describes the road to integrity: "There is a sense that one's life hasn't been, to borrow Macbeth's phrase, 'a tale told by an idiot . . . signifying nothing.' One doesn't look backward with a sense of existential disgust. The flavor of this period of life is now of discovery: who one was and what one did are reviewed; this is a phase of final consolidation. One can discern the shape and outline of what has been and examine the possibilities that remain, in terms of who one still may become."[146]

Scarf goes on to say that "this summing-up process can be an experience that throbs with pleasure and content-

ment—or it can be a mixed bag—or it can become exquisitely painful. For some people may, having been strapped
into the repetitive reconstruction of early childhood dilem-
mas, now confront the feeling that they've gone nowhere,
and done nothing, with their lives. It's been a waste . . . and
despair comes."[147]

For our woman, her contribution to society and to her
own immortality is largely completed. She must arrive at
some appraisal of her life. The task now is to gain a sense of
integrity in her life. If she can succeed in doing this, she
can then spend late adulthood without bitterness or despair. And by finding meaning and value in her life, however imperfect, she can come to terms with death.

Everyone feels despair at times, but Levinson reminds
us: "Whatever our values, we cannot live up to them fully.
In the end we must effect a reconciliation with the sources
of the flaws and corruptions in our lives. The sources are
multiple: they are in ourselves, in our enemies and in our
loved ones, in the imperfect world where each of us tries to
build a life of integrity. Making peace with all the enemies
in self and world is an important part of this task. To make
peace in this inner sense does not keep a person from fighting for one's convictions; but it does enable one to fight
with less rancor, with fewer illusions and with broader perspective."[148]

Scarf also talks about the despair that can occur in the
older years. She states: "A source of despair, in the sixties
and seventies, can proceed from a growing realization that
one has, in fact, gone round and round in one's life, in repeated attempts to solve a desperately significant riddle—
but that the riddle has never become articulated in such a
way that one could work on it, could find a stopping-place,
a solution. One's life story is approaching its conclusion;
and yet, in some deep way, the story hasn't gone forward:

the story of one's life feels hardly started." The grief and sense of waste that the older adult experiences now has to do with never quite having had it—the life that was, for want of a better word, authentic, in the sense that it was really one's own. "One has to be ready to be finished with having been, when one has never actually succeeded in getting to be. Death is approaching and one has, somehow, never gotten to live."[149]

But even aside from the developmental tasks involved in late adulthood, it is obvious that life for the elderly in the United States is indeed problematic. As a woman very interested in sociology, I have done extensive work in researching the field of aging in order to uncover the problems inherent in growing old in this country. This field is another of my special interests; I have always thought that younger Americans should and would be able to turn to our senior citizens for guidance since the wisdom of a lifetime of living should be in their possession.

If an individual has reached his "golden years" and developed to a higher level of consciousness, we should then see a person who has grown to a state of truth, wisdom and intuitive insight. We should see a person who has transcended his own self and is now consciously developed to a point where he is able to work interdependently in conjunction with other selves. Dr. Brian Hall described the self-transcended person. He points out that "the person sees the world as unfinished, its present constitution not nearly as important as its future potentiality. This viewpoint implies no disregard or lack of concern for existing persons or communities even though they too are viewed in their potentiality as much as in their actuality."

According to Hall, the world is seen as a mystery for which man now takes authority. The self-transcended man/woman chooses, creates and enhances the environment. That is to say that he/she takes authority over the creation and works in a cooperative manner with others and with nature itself in a common interdependent action seeking harmonious balance.[150]

If self-transcended persons do exist, it is most likely that we will find them in our older population who have lived long enough to have arrived at this state of consciousness development. Consequently, I find it deplorable that a country as technologically advanced as ours would define people according to production rather than what kinds of human beings they are. If ego autonomy and authentic living are capable of being achieved at all, it would be exhibited in senior citizens. But the structure of society prevents authentic living in old age by pushing the aged into a dependency role (the opposite of our definition of ego autonomy). As long as old age in America is viewed as a problem, political language, social values and public policies will reflect this belief. The concept of the aged as dependent and in need of services fosters the dependency attribution associated with receiving services.

One of my favorite quotes on the subject of America's treatment of the elderly comes from Robert Butler, currently the director of the National Institute on Aging and a long-time observer and participant in the lives of the aged, in his book, *Why Survive?*

> . . . but old age is frequently a tragedy even when the early years have been fulfilling and people seemingly have everything going for them. Herein lies what I consider to be the genuine tragedy of old age in America— we have shaped a society which is extremely harsh to live in when one is old. The tragedy of old age is not the fact that each of us must grow old and die, but that the process of doing so has been made unnecessarily

and at times excruciatingly painful, humiliating, debilitating and isolating through insensitivity, ignorance and poverty. The potentials for satisfaction and even triumphs in later life are real and vastly unexplored. For the most part the elderly struggle to exist in an inhospitable world.[151]

What about our woman in the winter of her life? The problems just mentioned may be more women's problems than men's, at least from a statistical point of view: of the almost twenty million older people (sixty-five and over) in the United States in 1970, eight million were men and over eleven million were women. By the year 2000, the ratio, as projected from today's growth factor, will be three women to every two men. These figures have great significance for our elderly woman, in every aspect of life—including the social, economic, and psychological. "Old age is indeed a woman's world and is becoming more so all the time."[152]

These facts have implications for the female, most of them negative. Could it be that, because such a high percentage of the elderly are women, this could account for society's treatment of them as children or obsolete persons who have simply outlived their usefulness? I would like to think not, but such a conclusion is not difficult to arrive at.

Sara Archer, in her article "The Double Challenge—To Be Old and To Be a Woman," has some excellent comments on women in the winter of their lives. She notes that society treats elderly women differently than men. This results in a different set of psychological and societal traumas and difficulties for women than exist for men as they age. She points out that, in general, women try to deny this "disease" of old age until it is no longer possible to do so. It seems that only women worry so much about aging. Today's society places a premium on youth for both sexes.

The man, however, commands respect, admiration, and even sexual enhancement as he matures.

Archer adds that the loss of physical beauty is the most obvious loss a woman experiences as she ages. Although men experience the apprehension and regret of aging and losing their boyish good looks, they do not experience the shame a woman feels. One of the differences is that men are given the leeway to be judged attractive in a mature manner. "A woman is too often judged by a criterion of beauty that can be met only during youth. Her life is spent in trying to conserve and create the illusion of youth with creams, cosmetics, and remedial exercises."[153]

American society frowns on ugly women, Archer states, and an old woman is almost by definition ugly. If an elderly woman is said to be beautiful it is because she does not look her chronological "real age." "Aging in women is a process of becoming obscene sexually; for the flabby bosom, wrinkled neck, spotted hands, thinning white hair, waistless torso, and veined legs of an old woman are felt to be obscene. By contrast, a man's face with its lines and wrinkles can be classified as a sign of character, with the lines denoting emotional strength and maturity."[154]

Dr. Robert Butler believes that very many older women are underemployed, underpaid, underfinanced, underhoused, undervalued, and underloved, sometimes even by themselves. He points out that because women live eight years longer than men and on the average are three years younger when they marry, women have ten or eleven years of widowhood. When an older retired man dies, that puts an end to his company pension; his widow then suffers poverty and loneliness and is prey to both physical assault and psychosomatic pain. Butler adds: "We live, after all, in a society which adds to its general rejection of the elderly a particular disdain for the older woman alone."[155]

Ruth Harriet Jacobs, in her article entitled "A Typology of Older American Women," lists thirteen different typologies of older women. Her information is of particular interest to us because she characterizes the different types of older women's roles. I will briefly describe the most important of these:

1. *Nurturers.* Nurturers have accepted traditional sex roles, and devote themselves to husband and kin as their primary or most salient activity. Jacobs notes that seventy-four percent of the women studied who had a high level of psychosomatic symptoms lived in traditional role settings and held traditional role stereotypes.

2. *Unemployed Nurturers.* These are women who have fulfilled a role as a homemaker and who find themselves "displaced" in later life through divorce, widowhood, or other loss of family income. Nurturers displaced by divorce are a high-risk group for suicide. This is often because suddenly the woman must live for herself and give up the role of "existing for others."

3. *Careerists.* Professional women find their primary satisfactions and their important social relations with other women. This is due to the proportion of older people being so heavily women. Careerists, though they may have husbands and kin, derive their main identity from work. While many older women continue in careers or re-enter them successfully, more could do the same were it not for prejudice, lack of adequate and inexpensive training, transportation problems, job shortages, etc.

4. *Advocates.* The skills and talents of these older women are employed in the service of various causes—political, environmental, feminist and others. Some of these women gain social status and a sense of importance as community leaders and in health and charitable campaigns.

The advocate role allows an opportunity for social interaction and ventilation of hostility.

5. *Escapists.* These include the women who drink too much. It is caused by the stresses of growing old, combined with loss of status, feelings of being useless, and loss of health. These stresses play a role in the deliberate misuse of drugs or alcohol in the aged woman. Drinking cliques may include women seeking relief from a painfully difficult environment. Bars, of course, are places for companionship.

6. *Assertive Seniors.* These women combine the advocate, nurturant, and career roles into an assertive senior role, working and fighting for their rights collectively. They nurture one another, fight ageism in society, and advocate legislation and programs that help older Americans.[156]

These are just a few of the roles that Jacobs mentions. Her feeling is that senior women, in order to be fulfilled, must engage in enriched multiple roles. But older women have very limited options and Jacobs believes that they especially suffer from the widespread faults of the society in general and from the very particular problems of ageism.

Further support for the older woman's need to function productively in society is provided by Philip Jaslow. He did an extremely interesting and relevant study which showed that older working women have better morale than those who do not work. His findings conclude that employment may tend to provide the older women—perhaps more than any other—with a source of dignity and self-esteem.

Jaslow also found that non-working women with virtually no employment history seem to be more demoralized in their later years than any other group of older women. He feels that this suggests that participation in the labor force may provide psychosocial benefits which carry over beyond retirement and into old age, thus tending to leave women better off for having had the experience than those whose lives have been entirely leisure-oriented.[157]

There are many new opportunities available to our woman as she goes through the winter of her life. Penelope Washbourn mentions some of these in her discussion of elderly women.

For the many women who have not had the opportunity for intellectual growth, old age provides them with the chance. "A woman can look to old age as a time to discover the parts of herself that have remained hidden, and she can at last speak for herself and herself alone."[158]

Becoming a widow can have some positive aspects. For some women widowhood liberates the self: "The creative journey in self-discovery and self-trust begins when a constructing interpretation of the role of oneself as a wife is finally left behind." The widow will need to find new comfort and strength in the company of other women. Living alone and being placed more extensively in the company of other women can be a destructive experience if our only understanding of being a woman is based on a relationship to a man. For this woman old age will mean having to find a new sense of herself as a woman not in relation to a man.[159]

Irene Claremont de Castellejo discusses the older woman who must now take the opportunity to reflect back on her life. She believes the older woman has the need and the obligation to tend the garden of the psyche. For it is in the latter part of life that people need to turn attention inward. She needs to do so because if her garden is as it should be she can die content, feeling that she has fulfilled her task of becoming the person she was born to be.

But de Castellejo believes that "being" is not the same as "doing." Most women have had to sacrifice in some direction their capacity to "do," but none are exempt from "being" to the full. The old woman who is frustrated and resentful because she has failed to become in life the person she should have become causes all in her vicinity to suffer.

There is no yardstick for the measurement of others, de Castellejo points out, but maybe for the woman herself there is. "Her yardstick is her full capacity to be as complete a person as within her lies, and that includes becoming as conscious as it is possible for her to be in order to bring out and develop the buried talents with which she was born and in order to realize her own innate knowledge."[160]

But becoming an "old hag" is a real possibility, Washbourn points out, because so many women have been socialized into believing that they are to live for others. These women spend their last years complaining and being bitter about all that they have suffered and all that they have missed. These are women who feel that they have been cheated of the opportunity to develop themselves intellectually and artistically. Having lived their lives exclusively in relation to husband and children, they are unable to find happiness in old age when these roles are left behind.[161]

Maggie Scarf talks about older women whose lives are empty. Something has gone wrong in their lives but there is no longer enough time to solve the problem. "And the problem, unresolved, was being experienced with a searing intensity: it was as though, at this point in their life, the psychological bill had come due with a burden of accrued interest; they had carried it over for too many decades, this bit of unfinished business."[162] She goes on to say that "for these women the past has been a sequence of disasters; the present is drab and hopeless, and the idea of the future dismal—but the idea of death, the death that felt nearer at this age, was absolutely terrorizing. It was as terrorizing, almost, as being alone; the two states were, in fact, indistinguishable."[163]

The winter of a woman's life is built upon the previous seasons and the woman's ability to find a creative sense of her own personal identity. If she never has developed a sense of ego autonomy, the winter is cold and barren. These "old women decline into despair, self-pity, and bitterness; their world shrinks around them as their perspective on themselves and their lives closes in. For such women old age is a living death; their spirits have already died, and there is no hope, no belief in themselves or in their ultimate significance to life to sustain them. Their days of usefulness to society are over, and they can find no value in the present day or in the years ahead. They look only backward to a self and a life that is now gone."[164]

The fact that so many women in the winter of their life have not accomplished Levinson's task of "individuation" is rather disheartening. The goal of adult personality development is ego autonomy, which occurs as a result of undergoing Levinson's process of individuation. Using a psychoanalytic theory of ego development, Jean Baker Miller believes that the ego, the "I" of psychoanalysis, may not be at all appropriate when talking about women. For women have different organizing principles around which their psyches are structured. One of these principles is that they exist to serve other people's needs. Few opportunities have existed in women's life for self-development and service to others simultaneously. Women have been said by many to have "more permeable ego structures" or "less rigid ego boundaries" than men.

Freud himself said that women have a less-developed super ego—a seeming disparagement. Miller pessimistically comments that prevailing psychoanalytic theories about women's weaker ego or superego may well reflect the concept that women have no ego or superego at all, as these terms are used now. Women do not come into this picture the way men do. Miller feels that women are not seen as having the right or requirement to be full-fledged representatives of the culture. Nor have they been granted the right to act and judge their own actions in terms of the direct benefit to themselves.[165]

Both of these rights seem essential to the development of ego and superego. "Women's reality is rooted in the encouragement to 'form' themselves into the person who will be of benefit to others. They thus see their own actions only as these actions are mediated through others. This experience begins at birth and continues through life. Out of it, women develop a psychic structuring for which the term ego, as ordinarily used, may not apply."[166]

Scarf says much the same thing. She opines that the female's self is more embedded in her important relationships. The embeddedness of women leads them to appear, when contrasted with men, more contextual in their sense of self, and more responsive to interpersonal cues. Scarf goes on to say that it should be recognized, however, that the woman's struggle to be autonomous, to be "me alone" and thoroughly capable of existing on her own, probably flies not only in the face of powerful feminine-behavior shaping—starting in earliest infancy—but of deep-seated biological tendencies as well.[167]

If the goals of adult life-cycle personality development are to achieve "ego autonomy" or "individuation," then we are forced to conclude that women have limited access to the achievement of these goals. It is important to think back on Carl Jung's definition of individuation: Individuation is the developmental process through which a person becomes more uniquely individual. A woman undergoing the process of individuation acquires a clearer and fuller identity of her own, and becomes better able to utilize her inner resources and pursue her own aims. Individuation is not without painful transitions and recurrent setbacks, but it holds the possibilities of continuing self-renewal and creative involvement in one's own life and the lives of others.[168]

The woman's "selfhood" has historically and presently hinged ultimately on other people's perceptions and evaluations, rather than her own. Male society, by depriving women of the right to its major "bounty"—that is, development according to the male model—overlooks the fact that women's development *is* proceeding, though on another basis. "One central feature is that women stay with, build on, and develop in a context of attachment and affiliation with others. Indeed, women's sense of self becomes very much organized around being able to make and then to maintain affiliations and relationships. Eventually, for many women, the threat of disruption of an affiliation is perceived as not just a loss of a relationship but as something closer to a total loss of self."[169]

This is, Scarf believes, where so much female depression begins. If one has been disappointed, then the real causes lie in one's own unacceptability, inferiority, unworthiness, unlovability, and guilt (guilt, especially, about underlying anger at the other). Becoming depressed is a way of discharging those awful, negative feelings, and yet leaving the needed emotional bond intact. The depressive stance is a waving of the white flag of powerlessness; and the bottom line, in the depressed female's contract, is that she will not be abandoned. It is a very bad bargain.[170]

Scarf believes that women, who are both taught to set such an enhanced value upon their emotional bonds and who are innately ready to learn to do so, enter the sea of modern adult realities in the leakiest of psychological ships. For having learned well the important lessons about the vital significance of love-bonds, and the ways in which her humanity and her being are to be defined by them, a woman must then make her way through an ocean of uncertainties in which her attachments may not indeed help to keep her afloat. Rupture and disintegration are not exceptions; they are cultural norms.[171] Just looking at the divorce statistics shows us that this is indeed so.

Our woman in the winter of her life has failed to achieve the male developmental goal of ego autonomy. It almost seems as if she were doomed from the start. The question we as women need to ask is: Why? It is absolutely imperative that this question be addressed because we need to understand the forces acting on and in women.

Some individuals are more optimistic about the prognosis for women. They believe that living in the 1980's has given women more options and that these problems confronting our woman in the winter of her life will cease to exist.

After all, we keep hearing that customs and expectations are changing and that young women are refusing marriage and motherhood in ever larger numbers. But statistics don't support this optimism. For the proportion of women who never marry has decreased over most of the last eighty years—from nine percent in the first decade of the century to seven percent in the seventh. Also, we see a remarkable decrease in childlessness as well—from almost fourteen percent of all married women in the early 1900's to just a little under four and a half percent in the present.[172]

In addition, the average age of entering a first marriage remains relatively unchanged—21.4 years in the early 1900's, 21.2 years in 1975. And most surprising of all is the fact that women who marry now are expected to be slightly younger when they bear their first child than they were eighty years ago.[173]

Consequently, it is not realistic to think that women growing up today will not be confronted with the same issues that we are now facing. It is my opinion that achievement of ego autonomy will continue to be problematic for women. For it will continue to be in terms of highly invested and extraordinarily important loving attachments that most women's secret self-assessments and interior appraisals of self-worth will be made.

It is important for women to understand the implications my conclusions suggest, not just for the sake of ourselves, but for the sake of future generations. If women continue to react solely out of ignorance there can be no chance for change. And it is ultimately social change that is my final goal, and the goal of others interested in women's human rights.

Conclusion

Our woman has passed through the seasons of her life without having achieved ego autonomy. One of the remaining questions is: Why not? Furthermore, what implications does this have for the future? The balance of this book will deal with these issues.

Causes for Non-Achievement of Ego Autonomy

What is the explanation for the position in which women find themselves today? I believe that there are a number of excellent theories on this; the first I will discuss is that of power structure analysis.

Those interested in the questions of power structure feel that we need to ask: Who benefits from female socialization? It is important to understand the profound significance of the socialization process by which girls and boys are prepared for their roles as women and men. But we must go further, sociologist Lillian Rubin says, and move beyond description of differential socialization to an analysis of the power structure that underlies that process and the institutional arrangements that buttress it. As Rubin states, from a sociological perspective we need to ask some core questions:

"Functional for whom? For what? The answer in unison: for the maintenance of the existing structure of power relations—whether in the economy, the polity, or the family."[174]

Many sociologists believe that women are victims of the power structure of the United States. For example, Kirsten Amundsen, in her book *A New Look at the Silenced Majority*, analyzes the power structure of American society to determine why women have failed to acquire access to positions of power.

She believes that sexism in the job market illustrates just how this power operates. Such sexism operates in two ways: (1) by confining women largely to the positions considered "suitable" for them, that is, the lesser-paid and lower-prestige positions; and (2) by limiting women to specific job classifications and production units within the businesses that hire both men and women. Occupation ceilings are set for women in nearly every instance. If women wish to advance they must be twice as good as men. Women are quite simply in a subordinate position, and it seems that they are meant to stay there.[175]

Amundsen goes on to say that it stands to reason that someone benefits from this situation. It is clear that women do not benefit, and it is far too easy an answer to point an accusing finger at men in general. Clearly, the husbands, fathers and sons have an interest in seeing the women of the family improve their present socio-economic state. While these men may wish that the woman would stay home and may express doubts in her ability, they aren't really deliberately striving to deprive her of higher earnings. And Amundsen also feels that the "common man" does not have much to do with decisions to hire or to fire, to raise wages and create benefits for workers. Sex prejudice is pervasive, but she doesn't feel that every man is equally responsible for the sexist differentiation in the job market. She believes that for the answer we must look at those empowered to make the decisions.

Amundsen believes that women's marginal positions in the economic system constitute the greatest reserve labor force in our society. The use of women as temporary workers, full or part time, is one of the most profitable arrangements available to employers in modern times. Amundsen suggests that this is a device to prevent any serious reordering of present structures and to allow the economy to expand and contract in response to new opportunities for the business elites, and not in response to the needs of workers.

One can also look at sex discrimination on the job. Why are women paid less for the same work a man does? Amundsen states: "The savings made possible by keeping women as a reserve labor force, although considerable, are as nothing compared to the profits to be had by continuing the lower wages offered women for work identical to that performed by men." During a Conference on Equal Pay, when asked why the pay of women in his factory was less than that of men, one employer replied: "Tradition, I suppose. . . . Anyhow, it's cheaper."[176]

Amundsen concludes that only the secondary status of women in American society and their exclusion from the major centers of power could make possible such continued and severe exploitation of a major portion of the labor force. Those who benefit are the business elites and no others.[177]

Jean Baker Miller also looks at women in terms of power. She sees power as reflected in the control which the dominant group exerts over the subordinate group. She believes that some people or groups of people are defined as unequal by means of what sociologists call ascription—that is, your birth defines you. Criteria may be race, sex, class, nationality, religion or other characteristics determined at birth.

Once a group is defined as inferior, superiors tend to label the group as defective or substandard in various ways. One such way is the supposition that women are ruled by emotion.

Miller states that dominant groups usually define one or more acceptable roles for the subordinate. And acceptable roles typically involve providing services that no dominant group wants to perform for itself. Subordinates are said to be unable to perform the preferred roles due to innate deficiencies of mind or body, therefore immutable and impossible to change or develop. (As a consequence, subordinates themselves can find it difficult to believe in their own ability.)[178]

Miller goes on to say that subordinates are described in terms of, and encouraged to develop, personal and psychological characteristics that are pleasing to the dominant group. These characteristics are submissiveness, passivity, docility, dependency, lack of initiative, inability to act, to decide, to think, etc. These qualities are more characteristic of children than adults—immaturity, weakness, and helplessness. If subordinates are able to adopt these characteristics, they are seen as well adjusted.

If the subordinates show the potential for or develop characteristics such as intelligence, initiative, and assertiveness, there is usually no room available within the dominant framework for acknowledgement of these characteristics. Such subordinates will be termed unusual and perhaps even abnormal.[179]

Miller mentions that dominant groups impede the development of subordinates and block their freedom of expression and action. And it is the dominant group that has the greatest influence in determining a culture's overall outlook—its philosophy, morality, social theory, etc. The dominant group legitimizes the unequal relationship and incorporates it into society's guiding concepts. The social outlook obscures the true nature of the relationship—the very existence of inequality. The culture will explain the events that take place in terms of other premises which are false, such as racial or sexual inferiority. For example, the belief that women are meant to be passive, submissive, docile and secondary has continued to exist in spite of overwhelming evidence to the contrary.[180]

Cynthia Fuchs Epstein also comments on power in America. She points out that value goals for the whole society seem to emanate from the upper stratum: "People of rank and prestige set the style; most typically people in the lesser positions tend to believe the goals of the powerful are the important ones, although they know they will be in no position to acquire them themselves. Because men are the rulers in all societies, the valued things and activities in most societies are the things men in power value."[181]

Epstein disagrees with those who say that women have no particular will, desire, or ambition for success. She believes that there is an "entrenched theoretical framework which underpins the assumptions that women don't want success or don't have the capacity to achieve it. That is, the set of ideas itself serves as a mechanism that keeps women in their place and out of the competition for the good things in life and keeps them from achieving power." She goes on to say: "Furthermore, the structure of our society works hand in glove with the structure of our thinking, resulting in the most minimal access to women."[182]

Lillian Rubin also discusses power. She believes that as long as women are in relationships where they are dependent they must be cautious. This is the nature between the powerful and the powerless. There is a threat implied in every request, sometimes intended, sometimes not. It doesn't matter. For so long as the threat is possible, so long as one person has the power to deprive another of important life supports, the powerless one experiences request as demand. "That is the psychology that accompanies powerlessness— indeed, is born of it. Whether among women, racial minor- ities, the poor of any color, even between parents and chil- dren, that psychology of powerlessness turns the relationship between the powerful and the powerless into a vicious circle from which escape is extremely difficult— possible perhaps only for the heroic and privileged few."[183]

Indeed, according to Rubin, we often point to these privileged ones to support the myth that equality exists and that it is some failure in the nature of the individual or of the entire group that is responsible for the deprivation we see. She states: "These exceptions, we say, prove the rule that we are a nation of equal opportunity for all, prove that competence, not color or sex, counts. In truth, such token- ism serves an important social function by taking the heat off the society and putting it on the individual, by provid- ing us with the rationale whereby we continue to blame the deprived for their deprivation."[184]

For women, their powerlessness is the fundamental fact upon which attitudes rest, upon which behavior grows—the fact that dominates their lives, whether con- sciously or unconsciously. It is an especially piercing fact of adult life, replaying as it does their earliest experiences in the family. Rubin tells us that in families, girls learn that efforts to separate can be dangerous—that there are power- ful others who block the path. Sometimes it's overt and di- rect—punishment, censure of one sort of another; more often it's covert and indirect—disapproval, withdrawal of affection. "Whichever the mode—one, both, or some combination of the two—they are effective tools for sending girls scurrying back to their place, properly chastened, properly subordinate and dependent."[185]

These early experiences of conflict around dependence–independence issues almost make it impossible for women to develop firm, separate personal boundaries. It is not simply that women carry these issues of separation, individuation, and independence from childhood into adulthood. But it is also that their adult lives and relationships replay these childhood ones. We see the same objective conditions, the same subjective ones.[186]

I heartily agree with Rubin that a girl child *could* develop a clear, bounded, and differentiated sense of self if she were raised in a culture and a family that valued her for it—that didn't make her fearful for her very survival whenever she moved in that direction. A woman could struggle successfully against the dependency and passivity for which a lifetime of being female has groomed her if the outcome of the struggle didn't threaten to doom her to a lifetime of loneliness and poverty.[187].

In reality, adult life is really a remarkable re-enactment of childhood—the interaction between her powerlessness, dependency, and need for emotional support essentially unchanged. The woman is left with the same old conflicts around independence, separation and individuation. These old conflicts are still acutely, painfully alive. Rubin states:

> She may rage, rebel, nag, become depressed. But each threat of withdrawal from a husband replays her earliest childhood fears when her moves toward separation and independence were met with similar responses from parents. Such interactions may leave her confused, frightened, perhaps angry, but, as in childhood, they bring her back—albeit ambivalently—into compli-

ance with the wishes of those on whom she must depend.[188]

Although I believe that power in America is structured in such a way as to keep women in an inferior position, I don't think that it is the whole answer to women's failure to achieve ego autonomy. Something else seems to be at work here. Since over half of the American population are women, they should have been able to make more progress toward equal rights and equal opportunities by this time in history. Some other force seems to be holding them back. Why is there such opposition by so many women to the passage of the Equal Rights Amendment? It's as if women themselves didn't really want to take their place alongside men as equals. I think that it is extremely important to ask ourselves why this is so.

Dorothy Dinnerstein provides us with some answers in her new book, *The Mermaid and the Minotaur.* Dinnerstein, a psychologist at Rutgers University, developed the underlying thesis of her book over a ten-year period: "The present sexual arrangements between men and women—that is, the division of rights, privileges and responsibilities that exist—are caused by the fact that all humans are mother-raised." What is important is the effect of predominantly female care on the later emotional predilections of the child. The point of crucial consequence, according to Dinnerstein, is that for virtually every living person it is a woman—usually the mother—who has provided the main initial contact with humanity and with nature.[189]

Under the present arrangements, a woman is the parental person who is every infant's first love, the person who presides over the infant's first encounters with the natural surroundings and who exists for the infant as the first representative of the flesh. The initial experience of dependence on a largely uncontrollable outside source of good is focused on a woman and so also is the earliest experience of vulnerability to disappointment and pain. Dinnerstein states: "This woman is the overwhelming external will in the face of which the child first learns the necessity for submission, the first being to whose wishes the child may be forced by punishment to subordinate its own, the first powerful and loved creature whom the child tries voluntarily to please."[190]

Dinnerstein believes that this is the cause of our species' fundamental ambivalence toward its female members. That early mother is a source like nature, a source of ultimate distress as well as ultimate joy. "Like nature, she is both nourishing and disappointing, both alluring and threatening, both comforting and unreliable." She goes on to state: "The mother, then—like nature, which sends blizzards and locusts as well as sunshine and strawberries—is perceived as capricious, sometimes actively malevolent."[191] She is the source of food, warmth and comfort; but the baby, no matter how well cared for, suffers from some hunger or cold, some aches and pains, some discomfort and some loneliness or boredom; and how is it to know that she is not the source of these too?

Consequently, the woman is inevitably forced into the dual role of indispensable quasi-human supporter and deadly quasi-human enemy of the human self. Every child thus finds it difficult to see that the magic parental presence of infancy was human, a person.[192]

This produces many problems for children as they grow up. Much of what males are trying to prove as they grow is that they are strong enough to withstand the kind of strength they imagine grown-up women possess. And females are trying to feel that they are really as grown-up, really as strong, as men imagine they are. Dinnerstein states:

> The fact that the infant's first extended encounter is with a woman, rather than with both a woman *and* a man, makes it in some ways harder to become a woman than a man. At the same time, it makes men in some ways more helpless with women than women are with men. The woman feels herself on the one hand a supernatural being, before whom the man bluffs, quails, struts, and turns stony for fear of melting; and she feels herself on the other hand a timid child, unable to locate in herself the full magic power which as a baby she felt in her mother. The man can seem to her to fit her childhood ideal of a male adult far better than she herself fits her childhood ideal of a female adult. This flaw in her sense of inner authority deepens from within a feeling of hers which society at the same time abundantly encourages from the outside: that she is unqualified for full worldly adult status; that she has no right to a voice in consequential public decisions; and therefore that she has no connection with the mainstream of human affairs except vicariously, through a man, so that without some personal alliance with him she can claim no formal place in human life.[193]

Dinnerstein concludes that as long as it is women who are mainly in charge of children the double standard will survive. "The harsh truth is that no societal compromise which changes other features of woman's condition while leaving her role as first parent intact will get at the roots of asymmetric sexual privilege."[194]

Dinnerstein believes there will be many problems in bringing about the desired social change that feminist women are insisting upon. "For it is one thing to want change in the educational, vocational, and legal status of women; but it is quite another thing to start tampering with Motherhood."[195]

Nancy Chodorow, a sociologist at the University of California at Santa Cruz, also has some rather profound comments in her book *The Reproduction of Mothering.* She draws upon the psychoanalytic account of female and male personality development in order to demonstrate that women's mothering reproduces itself cyclically. Her thesis is that "women, as mothers, produce daughters with mothering capacities and the desire to mother. These capacities and needs are built into and grow out of the mother-daughter relationship itself."[196] By contrast, women as mothers (and men as not-mothers) produce sons whose nurturant capacities and needs have been systematically curtailed and repressed.

Chodorow believes that the sexual and familial division of labor, in which the women mother and are more involved in the interpersonal, affective relationships, produces in daughters and sons a division of psychological capacities which leads them to further reproduce this sexual and familial division of labor.

Chodorow explains how women's mothering is reproduced: "Women's capacities for mothering and abilities to get gratification from it are strongly internalized and psychologically enforced, and are built developmentally into the feminine psychic structure. Women are prepared psychologically for mothering through the developmental situation in which they grow up, and in which women have mothered them."[197]

Both Chodorow and Dinnerstein believe that the only solution for women's current dilemma and for the improvement of women's status in society is to initiate and support co-parenting. Chodorow tells us that if our goal is to overcome the sexual division of labor in which women mother, we need to understand the mechanism which reproduces it in the first place. Her account points precisely to where intervention should take place. "Any strategy whose goal includes liberation from the constraints of an unequal social organization of genders must take account of the need for a fundamental reorganization of parenting, so that primary parenting is shared between men and women."[198]

I believe that both Chodorow's and Dinnerstein's analyses add much to explaining why women's situation has not improved significantly, even though over half this country's population is made up of women. Their illuminating works help us to understand why the seasons of a woman's life are different in some very fundamental respects from the seasons of life for the men in Levinson's study. While I believe it is necessary to analyze the power structure of a society in order to determine who benefits from certain inequities, I don't feel that this provides an adequate explanation for the inequality facing women today. I believe that a combination of psychological and sociological reasons, such as those stated above, best gives the answers to the questions which this book has posed.

Implications for the Future

Sex-role stereotyping is very pervasive in our society. And to the extent that Levinson is providing and articulating societal developmental norms, women who do not complete the developmental tasks he outlines must inevitably view themselves (and be viewed by others) as failing to achieve full adult status. But ultimately the true liberation of the American woman will require a society structured quite differently than America is right now. What is needed is a society where arrangements are made to insure the realization and utilization of the potential of *every* human being.

Many sexist myths do prevail, and they will continue to do so as long as women are misperceived and maligned in the cliché-ridden views conjured up by the media. I believe that the exposure of the ways sexism is being fostered in our country will ultimately lead to the destruction of these false myths.

Knowledge can be power. Feminists are working diligently to expose the inequities. Also, social analysts have recently become interested in examining the social forces at work behind the relations between the sexes. Besides the illuminating works of Chodorow and Dinnerstein, referred to above, sociologist Erving Goffman has recently published a book on "depicted femininity." His book, *Gender Advertisements*, shows us the ways in which men and women—mainly women—are pictured in advertisements. Expositions such as Goffman's can accomplish a great deal in raising the consciousness of both men and women.

Goffman's work illustrates how advertisements depict not necessarily how we *actually* behave as men and women but how we *think* men and women behave. And this depiction serves the social purpose of convincing us that this is how men and women are, or want to be, or should be, not only in relation to themselves, but in relation to each other.[199]

Goffman has displayed in his book many of these advertisements. Along with the pictures is a running commentary that clearly demonstrates that while the advertisements appear to be photographing male and female human beings, what they are actually photographing is a depiction of masculinity and femininity which are fitted or matched in such a way as to make them function socially.[200]

Goffman's work is a masterpiece, and I believe that social change ultimately results from such efforts. Goffman brilliantly points out such observable phenomena in advertising as the following:

1. Invariably the man is taller than the woman, except when the man is her social inferior.

2. A woman's hands are usually seen just barely touching, holding or caressing—rarely grasping, manipulating or shaping.

3. When a photograph of men and women illustrates an instruction of some sort, the man is typically instructing the woman.

4. When an advertisement requires someone to sit or lie on a bed or a floor, that someone is almost always a child or a woman, hardly ever a man.

5. Women are repeatedly pictured as mentally drifting from the scene, their faces lost and dreamy, while in close physical touch with a male, "as though his aliveness to the surroundings and his readiness to cope were enough for both of them."[201]

Goffman's illustrations enable us to see the connection between our image of women and the behavior of children. We see the repeated usage in advertisements of women posed as children, acting like children, looking like children—utterly devoid of the natural sobriety which one associates with the adult mien.[202]

Goffman's book will definitely serve as a "consciousness raiser." And as more women are made aware of the problems that need to be dealt with, the more progress we will see. The common images of women and their proper roles in society will have to be changed, and I believe it is ultimately through the education of women that we will accomplish this task. It is an imperative that we continue to fight the "benign neglect," the stubborn refusal to face the social and economic realities confronting American women.

Also, I am hopeful that Chodorow's and Dinnerstein's exposure of the problems inherent in the female's sole responsibility for early child-care will hopefully contribute to situations of co-parenting—which I believe will ultimately bring about the needed social change. As Chodorow states:

> The elimination of the present organization of parenting in favor of a system in which both men and women are responsible would be a tremendous social advance. This outcome is historically possible, but far from inevitable. Such advances do not occur simply because they are better for "society" and certainly not simply because they are better for some (usually less powerful) people. They depend on the conscious organization and activity of all women and men who recognize that their interests lie in transforming the social organization of gender and eliminating sexual inequality.[203]

Ideal images of male and female seem to be changing consistently in the direction of emphasizing the androgynous possibilities in personality. One task of Levinson's individuation process is to achieve a balance between the masculine and feminine qualities in ourselves. Our world view, however, is not yet structured to permit easy incorporation of these new images. New historical and cross-cultural research reveals a gradual transformation of consciousness whereby human beings now have a great opportunity—greater than at any time in the past—not to have their lives limited by the fact of their biological gender.

Janet Giele points out in *Woman and the Future* that in the last analysis it is the individual who filters the cultural elements that are currently in a state of ferment. Psychologists find that past stereotyping of sex roles has caused considerable suffering for both sexes. Men have had to deny their emotionality; women, their own self-direction. But developments in biology, psychology, and sociology are presently converging on a new model of adult behavior in which both masculine and feminine aspects are present. Men who are strong and assertive may also be tender and caring. Women who are sensitive and devoted to others may also pursue their own interests.[204]

Giele feels that the realization of this new adult ideal has been made possible by the increase in life expectancy. Life that would have ended with an "early death" can now be used to explore the unrealized potentials within the self. But further expression of both "male" and "female" qualities and behaviors awaits slow and incremental changes in social structures.

I agree with Giele that when more and more women are brought into the workplace, their self-direction and self-confidence will be strengthened. As men give more time to child-rearing and child-care, their own nurturant qualities will be reinforced, and they will help to form a generation in which sex differences will be attenuated.[205]

Women must come to realize just where their "dependency needs" originated and they must be educated to understand that as long as they are solely dependent on emotional attachments, their own ego development will be stymied. Too often women feel like the woman quoted below.

> So the question is, if masochism is out as a way of life; if it is no longer a worthy calling; if, in fact, it is nothing but a sickness—then what do I do with my years of training? I'm not really fitted for any other kind of relationship. I'm not even convinced there is another kind.[206]

Jean Baker Miller believes that it is really around the issue of power that aspects of feminine masochism revolve. It is often much easier to be, and remain, the victim than to struggle for oneself. Miller states:

> For even in a situation that is objectively destructive, the victim does not have to confront her own desires to change the situation, her own power to do so, nor the anger that has mounted and accumulated over her victimized position. It can seem easier to blame the other person and thus protect oneself from dealing with these difficult issues. Since society so firmly encourages women to remain in this position, moving out of it means working against very heavy odds. To attempt to change the situation threatens women with no place to go, no alternatives, and, worst of all, total isolation and complete condemnation. Such threats can be well validated by reality, then recycled to reconfirm women's already deeply internalized fears.[207]

Miller goes on to say that blaming the person(s) who hurt you can seem much harder than continuing the masochistic circle of self-condemnation. This is especially true if the woman believes that the other person is absolutely necessary to her very existence. "A masochistic person may seem to blame the oppressor; but she blames herself even more, and the situation is never changed for either person."

I heartily agree with Miller that all of the valuable qualities that women do have—like helping in the development of others—will not provide them with a self-determined, authentic, effective life. The characteristics most highly developed in women and perhaps the most essential to human beings are the very characteristics that are specifically dysfunctional in the world as it exists today.[208]

We, as women, are beginning to realize these painful

truths. Lillian Rubin calls the woman who has solely dedicated her life to the service of others the "woman who has no name." She states:

> She's one of us; and she's all of us—all the women we have known for so long; all of them who have been John's wife, Stephanie's mother, the Barnetts' daughter; all the women who, until now, have had no name. She still exists, this woman who has no name. She's the woman who lives in the house down the street. And the one who lives on the hill. But whoever she is, wherever she lives, she's beginning now to be aware of the loss, beginning now to count up the cost. And from the pain she's finding deep in her soul, the words well up in a shout: The world makes it hard, not me. Tell them that, will you—TELL THEM![209]

Women do have choices. We can choose to add new dimensions to our existing vision of womanhood. It is my belief that the seasons of a woman's life offer each woman a unique challenge. She can use each season as an opportunity for growth, or she can allow the societal obstacles within these seasons to hinder her development. For a woman to cope with these seasons, she must understand the intricacies involved in each of them, and she must understand that she has the freedom to either rechoose her ancient roles or create a set of new ones. "If a woman understands the inner constellation of her problem as well as the nature of her humanity and her femininity, she will thereby have acquired the will to act in her own eventual best interest. Since the most any philosophical or psychological position can offer is insight, the motivation for action remains the natural corollary of right knowledge."[210]

Women can change. Many women are now in a situation where they no longer simply accept the duties and obligations traditionally assigned to them. Women have a responsibility to create an atmosphere where they can learn together, deal with their problems together, and act collectively in their struggle to assume their rightful position as authentic and fully functioning adults in the world.

> Becoming women is not a process that is ever finished. . . . The task of finding oneself is never completed, but each stage of life brings its own possibilities for renewal and joy and sorrow. There is no fixed female identity. One element of a false solution to life is to stagnate in one identity, one stage, one self-image of womanhood. Each of us is many women, and each stage of life offers the potential for discovering new freedom and new growth. . . . Sometimes we despair that nothing can be done; we have been determined by our childhood, our society, our culture, our age, and there is no hope. . . . But ultimately a woman's life is her own; she is free to live gracefully or demonically right to the last.
>
> Becoming woman is a spiritual search. It involves finding a sense of one's personal worth in relation to the whole of life. . . . Believing in ourselves, loving ourselves as women, is our most sacred task. . . . Finding freedom from fear involves risking and trusting our feelings. As we risk, however, we will be given new hope, new strength, and a new love for ourselves and others. Acting on this trust will enable us to grow in understanding through all the stages of life.[211]

Notes

1. Daniel Levinson, *The Seasons of a Man's Life* (New York: Alfred A. Knopf, Inc., 1978), p. 330.

2. *Ibid.*, p. 2.

3. *Ibid.*, p. 42.

4. *Ibid.*

5. *Ibid.*

6. *Ibid.*, p. 322.

7. *Ibid.*, p. 323.

8. Group for the Advancement of Psychiatry (GAP), *The Educated Woman* (New York: Charles Scribners & Sons, 1975), p. 149.

9. *Ibid.*

10. Levinson, p. 49.

11. Penelope Washbourn, *Becoming Woman* (New York: Harper & Row, 1977), p. 21.

12. *Ibid.*

13. *Ibid.*, p. 23.

14. *Ibid.*

15. Lois Vladis Hoffman, "Early Childhood Experiences and Women's Achievement Motives," *Journal of Social Issues*, Vol. 28, Number 2 (1972), p. 147.

16. *Ibid.*, p. 149.

17. *Ibid.*, p. 159.

18. Matina S. Horner, "Toward An Understanding of

Achievement-Related Conflicts in Women," *Journal of Social Issues*, Vol. 28, Number 2 (1972), p. 179.

19. Kirsten Amundsen, *A New Look at the Silenced Majority* (Englewood Cliffs, N.J.: Prentice-Hall, Inc., 1977), p. 111.

20. *Ibid.*

21. Levinson, p. 9.

22. Peter Koestenbaum, *The Vitality of Death* (Westport, Conn.: Greenwood Press, Inc., 1971), p. 146.

23. *Ibid.*, p. 147.

24. Washbourn, p. 81.

25. *Ibid.*, p. 82.

26. *Ibid.*

27. Edwin Lewis, *Developing Woman's Potential* (Ames, Iowa: Iowa State University Press, 1968), p. 155.

28. *Ibid.*, p. 157.

29. *Ibid.*

30. *Ibid.*

31. Wendy Ann Steward, "A Psychosocial Study of the Formation of the Early Adult Life Structure in Women" (Diss., Columbia University, 1977), p. 119.

32. GAP, p. 121.

33. Steward, p. 96.

34. Maggie Scarf, *Unfinished Business* (New York: Doubleday & Co., 1980), p. 225.

35. *Ibid.*, p. 226.

36. *Ibid.*, p. 227.

37. Amundsen, pp. 114–115.

38. Levinson, p. 71.

39. Steward, p. 9.

40. Barbara Marx Hubbard, *The Hunger of Eve* (Harrisburg, Pa.: Stackpole Books, 1976), p. 27.

41. Washbourn, p. 82.

42. Steward, p. 78.

43. *Ibid.*, p. 45.

44. *Ibid.*, p. 68.

45. *Ibid.*, p. 55.

46. *Ibid.*, p. 64.

47. *Ibid.*, p. 77.

48. *Ibid.*, p. 88.

49. *Ibid.*, p. 101.

50. *Ibid.*

51. Lillian Rubin, *Women of a Certain Age* (New York: Harper & Row, 1979), p. 130.

52. *Ibid.*

53. *Ibid.*, p. 132.

54. *Ibid.*, p. 208.

55. Washbourn, p. 82.

56. *Ibid.*, p. 83.

57. *Ibid.*, p. 84.

58. Irene Claremont de Castillejo, *Knowing Woman* (New York: Harper & Row, 1973), p. 41.

59. Peter Koestenbaum, "The New Image of the Person: Loneliness, Love, Reality" (Paper presented at the Western Regional Meeting, Association for Humanistic Psychology, February 2, 1979), p. 10.

60. Nancy Chodorow, *The Reproduction of Mothering* (Berkeley: University of California Press, 1978), p. 212.

61. *Ibid.*, p. 217.

62. Steward, p. 9.

63. *Ibid.*, p. 103.

64. Barbara J. Estes, "A Descriptive Study of the Developmental Phase of Women in Their 30's" (Diss., University of Pittsburgh, 1977), p. 58.

65. *Ibid.*, p. 59.

66. *Ibid.*, p. 64.

67. *Ibid.*

68. *Ibid.*, pp. 67–68.

69. Jean Baker Miller, *Toward a New Psychology of Women* (Boston: Beacon Press, 1976), p. 114.

70. *Ibid.*, p. 110.

71. *Ibid.*

72. Koestenbaum, *Vitality of Death*, p. 150.

73. *Ibid.*

74. De Castillejo, p. 150.

75. Levinson, p. 192.

76. *Ibid.*, pp. 192–193.

77. *Ibid.*, p. 192.

78. *Ibid.*

79. *Ibid.*, p. 194.

80. *Ibid.*, p. 196.

81. *Ibid.*

82. *Ibid.*, p. 217.

83. *Ibid.*, p. 210.

84. Scarf, p. 486.

85. Levinson, p. 222.

86. *Ibid.*, p. 224.

87. Peter Koestenbaum, *The New Image of the Person* (Westport, Conn.: Greenwood Press, 1978), p. 206.

88. Levinson, p. 239.

89. *Ibid.*

90. *Ibid.*, p. 240.

91. Scarf, p. 535.

92. Levinson, p. 243.

93. *Ibid.*

94. *Ibid.*, p. 278.

95. *Ibid.*

96. *Ibid.*, p. 279.

97. Maggie Scarf, "The More Sorrowful Sex," *Psychology Today*, Vol. 12, Number 11 (April 1979), p. 47.

98. *Ibid.*

99. *Ibid.*, p. 48.

100. Rubin, p. 185.

101. *Ibid.*

102. *Ibid.*

103. Scarf, "The More Sorrowful Sex," p. 48.

104. *Ibid.*, p. 51.

105. *Ibid.*

106. *Ibid.*

107. Claudeen Cline-Naffziger, "Women's Lives and Frustration, Oppression, and Anger: Some Alternatives," *Journal of Counseling Psychology* 21, No. 1 (1974), p. 52.

108. Scarf, *Unfinished Business,* p. 98.

109. *Ibid.,* p. 537.

110. Scarf, "The More Sorrowful Sex," p. 52.

111. *Ibid.,* p. 54.

112. Cline-Naffziger, p. 55.

113. *Ibid.*

114. Koestenbaum, *New Image,* p. 258.

115. Cline-Naffziger, p. 55.

116. Estes, p. 77.

117. Washbourn, p. 134.

118. *Ibid.*

119. Florine B. Livson, "Patterns of Personality Development in Middle-Aged Women: A Longitudinal Study," *International Journal of Aging and Human Development,* Vol. 7 (1976), p. 108.

120. Levinson, pp. 62–63.

121. Juanita H. Williams, *Psychology of Women: Behavior in a Biosocial Context* (New York: W. W. Norton & Co., 1977), p. 355.

122. *Ibid.,* p. 356.

123. *Ibid.,* p. 357.

124. *Ibid.,* p. 356.

125. *Ibid.,* p. 357.

126. De Castillejo, p. 152.

127. *Ibid.*

128. *Ibid.*

129. Scarf, *Unfinished Business,* p. 397.

130. *Ibid.,* p. 410.

131. *Ibid.,* p. 412.

132. Joan Z. Cohen, Karen Levin Coburn, and Joan Pearlman, *Hitting Our Stride* (New York: Delacorte Press, 1980), p. 179.

133. Miller, p. 111.

134. *Ibid.,* p. 112.

135. Lillian Troll, Joan Israel, and Kenneth Israel, *Looking Ahead* (New Jersey: Prentice-Hall Inc., 1977), p. 186.

136. Anna Regula Herzog, "Attitude Change in Older Age:

An Experimental Study," *Journal of Gerontology*, Vol. 34, No. 5, Sept. 1979, p. 702.

137. Scarf, *Unfinished Business*, p. 420.

138. Williams, p. 364.

139. Troll, Israel, and Israel, p. 178.

140. *Ibid.*, p. 179.

141. Levinson, p. 34.

142. *Ibid.*, pp. 62–63.

143. De Castillejo, p. 150.

144. Levinson, p. 34.

145. *Ibid.*, p. 36.

146. Scarf, *Unfinished Business*, p. 468.

147. *Ibid.*, p. 486.

148. Levinson, p. 38.

149. Scarf, *Unfinished Business*, p. 488.

150. Brian P. Hall, *The Development of Consciousness* (New York: Paulist Press, 1976), p. 76.

151. C. L. Estes, "Political Gerontology," *Society*, Vol. 15 (July 1978), p. 48.

152. Sara K. Archer, "The Double Challenge—To Be Old and to Be a Woman," *Soundings*, Vol. 57 (Spring 1974), p. 51.

153. *Ibid.*, p. 53.

154. *Ibid.*

155. Ruth Harriet Jocobs, "A Typology of Older American Women," *Social Policy* (November/December 1976), p. 34.

156. *Ibid.*, pp. 34–38.

157. Philip Jaslow, "Employment, Retirement, and Morale Among Older Women," *Journal of Gerontology*, Vol. 31, Number 2 (March 31, 1976), p. 217.

158. Washbourn, p. 147.

159. *Ibid.*

160. De Castillejo, p. 159.

161. Washbourn, p. 151.

162. Scarf, *Unfinished Business*, p. 487.

163. *Ibid.*, p. 489.

164. Washbourn, p. 143.

165. Miller, p. 71.

166. *Ibid.*, p. 72.

167. Scarf, *Unfinished Business*, p. 536.

168. Levinson, p. 33.

169. Miller, p. 83.

170. Scarf, *Unfinished Business*, p. 536.

171. *Ibid.*

172. Rubin, p. 8.

173. *Ibid.*, p. 9.

174. *Ibid.*, p. 86.

175. Amundsen, p. 32.

176. *Ibid.*, p. 56.

177. *Ibid.*, p. 58.

178. Miller, p. 7.

179. *Ibid.*

180. *Ibid.*, p. 9.

181. Cynthia Fuchs Epstein, "Separate and Unequal: Notes on Women's Achievement," *Social Policy* (March/April 1976), p. 17.

182. Epstein, p. 18.

183. Rubin p. 153.

184. *Ibid.*

185. *Ibid.*, p. 154.

186. *Ibid.*

187. *Ibid.*

188. *Ibid.*

189. Dorothy Dinnerstein, *The Mermaid and the Minotaur* (New York: Harper & Row, 1977), p. 26.

190. *Ibid.*, p. 29.

191. *Ibid.*, p. 95.

192. *Ibid.*, p. 112.

193. *Ibid.*, pp. 85–86.

194. *Ibid.*, p. 76.

195. *Ibid.*

196. Chodorow, p. 7.

197. *Ibid.*, p. 39.

198. *Ibid.*, pp. 214–215.

199. Erving Goffman, *Gender Advertisements* (New York: Harper & Row, 1979), p. viii.

200. *Ibid.*

201. *Ibid.*

202. *Ibid.*

203. Chodorow, p. 219.

204. Janet Zollinger Giele, *Women and the Future* (London: Collier Macmillan Publishers, 1978), p. 359.

205. *Ibid.,* p. 368.

206. Rubin, p. 213.

207. Miller, p. 122.

208. *Ibid.,* p. 124.

209. Rubin, p. 213.

210. Koestenbaum, *Vitality of Death,* p. 150.

211. Washbourn, p. 155.

Bibliography

Books

Amundsen, Kirsten. *A New Look at the Silenced Majority.* New Jersey: Prentice-Hall, Inc., 1977.

Bardwick, Judith M. *Psychology of Women.* New York: Harper & Row, 1971.

Chodorow, Nancy. *The Reproduction of Mothering.* Berkeley: University of California Press, 1978.

Cohen, Joan Z., Karen Levin Coburn, and Joan Pearlman. *Hitting Our Stride.* New York: Delacorte Press, 1980.

De Castillejo, Irene C. *Knowing Woman.* New York: Harper & Row, 1977.

Dinnerstein, Dorothy. *The Mermaid and the Minotaur—Sexual Arrangements and Human Malaise.* New York: Harper & Row, 1977.

Friday, Nancy. *My Mother/My Self.* New York: Dell, 1978.

Fried, Barbara. *The Middle Age Crisis.* New York: Harper & Row, 1967.

Friedan, Betty. *The Feminine Mystique.* New York: Dell, 1963.

Garskof, Michele H., ed. *Roles Women Play.* Belmont, California: Brooks-Cole Publishing Co., Inc., 1971.

Giele, Janet Zollinger. *Women and the Future.* London: Collier Macmillan Publishers, 1978.

Goffman, Erving. *Gender Advertisements.* New York: Harper & Row, 1979.

Gornick, Vivian, and Barbara Moran, eds. *Woman in Sexist Society.* New York: Basic Books Inc., 1971.

Gould, Roger L. *Transformations: Growth and Change In Adult Life.* New York: Simon and Schuster, 1978.

Group for the Advancement of Psychiatry. *The Educated Woman.* New York: Charles Scribner's Sons, 1975.

Hall, Brian P. *The Development of Consciousness.* New York: Paulist Press, 1976.

Hubbard, Barbara Marx. *The Hunger of Eve.* Harrisburg: Stackpole Books, 1976.

Koestenbaum, Peter. *The New Image of the Person.* Westport, Conn.: Greenwood Press, 1978.

———. *The Vitality of Death.* Westport, Conn.: Greenwood Press, 1971.

Levinson, Daniel. *The Seasons of a Man's Life.* New York: Alfred Knopf, 1978.

Lewis, Edwin. *Developing Women's Potential.* Ames, Iowa: Iowa State University Press, 1968.

Lowenthal, Marjorie, Majda Thurher, and David Chriboga. *Four Stages of Life.* San Francisco: Jossey-Bass, Inc., 1975.

Miller, Jean Baker. *Toward a New Psychology of Women.* Boston: Beacon Press, 1976.

Neugarten, Bernice, ed. *Middle Age and Aging: A Reader in Social Psychology.* Chicago: University of Chicago, 1968.

Reeves, Nancy. *Womankind.* Chicago: Aldine-Atherton, Inc., 1971.

Rothman, Sheila. *Woman's Proper Place: A History of Changing Ideals and Practices, 1890 to the Present.* New York: Basic Books, Inc., 1978.

Rubin, Lillian B. *Women of a Certain Age.* New York: Harper & Row, 1979.

———. *Worlds of Pain.* New York: Basic Books, Inc., 1976.

Scarf, Maggie. *Unfinished Business.* New York: Doubleday & Co., Inc., 1980.

Sheehy, Gail. *Passages.* New York: Dutton, 1976.

Troll, Lillian, Joan Israel, and Kenneth Israel. *Looking Ahead.* New Jersey: Prentice-Hall Inc., 1977.

Vaillant, George. *Adaptation to Life.* Boston: Little, Brown, & Co., 1977.

Washbourn, Penelope. *Becoming Woman.* New York: Harper & Row, 1977.

Williams, Juanita H. *Psychology of Women: Behavior in a Biosexual Context.* New York: W. W. Norton & Co., 1977.

Dissertations

Estes, Barbara J. "A Descriptive Study of the Developmental Phase of Women in Their 30's." Diss., University of Pittsburgh, 1977.

Steward, Wendy Ann. "A Psychosocial Study of the Formation of the Early Adult Life Structure in Women." Diss., Columbia University, 1977.

Articles

Archer, Sara Katherine. "The Double Challenge—To Be Old and To Be a Woman." *Soundings* 57, Spring 1974, pp. 50–69.

Arlin, P. K. "Cognitive Development in Adulthood: A Fifth Stage." *Developmental Psychology* 12, Sept. 1976, pp. 602–606.

Arling, Gregory. "Resistance to Isolation Among Elderly Widows." *International Journal of Aging and Human Development* 7 (1976), pp. 67–86.

Bartky, S. L. "Toward a Phenomenology of Feminist Consciousness." *Social Theory and Practice* 3, No. 4 (1975), pp. 425–439.

Bedeian, Arthur and John Touliatos. "Work-Related Motives and Self-Esteem in American Women." *The Journal of Psychology* 99, May 1978, pp. 63–70.

Beeson, Diane. "Women in Studies of Aging: A Critique and Suggestion." *Social Problems* 23, April 1976, pp. 52–59.

Berkum, C., *et al.* "Women's Issues." *Social Work,* Nov. 22, 1977, pp. 502+.

Booth, A. "Wife's Employment and Husband's Stress: A Replication and Refutation." *Journal of Marriage and Family* 39, Nov. 1977, pp. 645–656.

Brieland, D. "Volunteering and the Worth of Experience." *Social Work* 22, March 1977, pp. 86–98.

Brody, S. J. "Public Policy Issues of Women in Transition." *Gerontologist* 16, April 1976, pp. 181–183.

Brubaker, T. H. "Sex-Role Expectations Associated with Specific Household Tasks: Perceived Age and Employment Differences." *Psychological Reporter* 41, Aug. 1977, pp. 15–18.

Burns, M. S. A. "Life Styles for Women, An Attitude Scale." *Psychological Reporter* 35, Aug. 1974, pp. 227–237.

Butler, M. A. "Early Liberal Roots of Feminism: John Locke and the Attack on Patriarchy." *American Political Science Review* 72, March 1978, pp. 135–150.

Cantor, P. C. "Personality Characteristics Found Among Youthful Suicide Attempters." *Journal of Abnormal Psychology* 85, June 1976, pp. 324–329.

Carlson, R. "Understanding Women: Implications for Personality Theory and Research." *Journal of Social Issues* 28 (1972), pp. 17–32.

"Change in Life Satisfaction." *Journal of Gerontology* 32, May 1977, pp. 311–316.

Clark, Shirley. "Women's Behavior Manifestations of Traditionalist and Liberated Role Concepts." *Journal of Psychology* 98, Jan. 1978, pp. 81–89.

Clausen, John A. "The Social World of Middle-Age." *International Journal of Aging and Human Development* 7, No. 2 (1976), pp. 99–106.

Clifton-Mogg, C. "Ashley Montagu on the Superiority of Women (Interview)." *Business and Society Review,* No. 25, Spring 1978, pp. 35–42.

Cline-Naffziger, Claudeen. "Women's Lives and Frustration, Oppression, and Anger: Some Alternatives." *Journal of Counseling Psychology* 21, No. 1 (1974), pp. 51–56.

Cohen, P. M. "Factor Analytic Examination of Role Attitudes of Married Women." *Psychological Reporter* 42, April 1978, pp. 423–434.

Coleman, R. E. "Manipulation of Self-Esteem as a Determinant of Mood of Elated and Depressed Women." *Journal of Abnormal Psychology* 84, Dec. 1975, pp. 693–700.

Darian, J. C. "Factors Influencing the Rising Labor Force Participation Rates of Married Women with Pre-School Children." *Social Science Quarterly* 56, March 1976, pp. 614–630.

Dye, N. and H. J. Fine. "Concept of Character Revisited: An Ego-Psychological View with Some Thoughts on the Depressive Character." *Psychological Reporter* 41, Dec. 1977, pp. 763–776.

Epstein, Cynthia Fuchs. "Separate and Unequal: Notes on Women's Achievement." *Social Policy,* March/April 1976, pp. 17–23.

Ericksen, J. A. "Analysis of the Journey to Work for Women." *Social Problems* 24, April 1977, pp. 428–435.

Estes, C. L. "Political Gerontology." *Society* 15, July 1978, pp. 43–49.

Ferree, Myra. "Working Class Jobs: Housework and Paid-Work as Sources of Satisfaction." *Social Problems* 23, April 1976, pp. 431–441.

Follingstad, D. R. "Effects of Consciousness-Raising Groups on Measures of Feminism, Self-Esteem, and Social Desirability." *Journal of Counseling Psychology* 24, May 1977, pp. 223–230.

Fox, Judith. "Effects of Retirement and Former Work-Life on Women's Adaption in Old Age." *Journal of Gerontology* 32, March 1977, pp. 196–202.

Fry, C. L. "Ages of Adulthood: A Question of Numbers." *Journal of Gerontology* 31, March 1976, pp. 170–177.

Halleck, S. L. "Family Therapy and Social Change." *Social Casework* 57, Oct. 1976, pp. 483–493.

Hardison, N. M. and D. J. Vanier. "Age as a Determinant of Sex-Role Stereotyping." *Psychological Reporter* 42, Feb. 1978, pp. 35–38.

Harkins, Elizabeth B. "Effects of Empty Nest Transition and Physical Well-Being." *Journal of Marriage and Family*, August 1978, pp. 549–555.

Haun, Norma. "Personality Organization of Well-Functioning Younger People and Older Adults." *International Journal of Aging and Human Development* 7 (1976), pp. 117–127.

Heide, W. S. "Women's Work: Remaking Society." *Social Policy* 8, May 1977, pp. 46+.

Herzog, Anna Regula. "Attitude Change in Older Age: An Experimental Study." *Journal of Gerontology* 34, No. 5, Sept. 1979, pp. 697–703.

Hjelle, L. A. and R. Butterfield. "Self-Actualization and Women's Attitudes Toward Their Roles in Contemporary Society." *Journal of Psychology* 87, July 1974, pp. 225–230.

Hoffman, Lois Wladis. "Early Childhood Experiences and Women's Achievement Motives." *Journal of Social Issues* 28, No. 2 (1972), pp. 129–151.

Hoffman, Saul. "Marital Instability and the Economic Status of Women." *Demography* 14, No. 1, Feb. 1977, pp. 67–77.

Hogan, Dennis P. "Variable Order of Events in Life Course." *American Sociological Review* 43, August 1978, pp. 573–586.

Horner, Matina S. "Bright Woman Is Caught in a Double Bind." *Psychology Today* 3, Nov. 1969, pp. 52+.

———. "Toward an Understanding of Achievement-Related Conflicts in Women." *Journal of Social Issues* 28, No. 2 (1972) pp. 157–180.

Howarth, E. "Personality Characteristics of Volunteers." *Psychological Reporter* 38, June 1976, pp. 855–858.

Hunter, J. E. "Images of Women." *Journal of Social Issues* 32 (1976), pp. 7–17.

Jacobs, Ruth Harriet. "A Typology of Older American Women." *Social Policy*, November/December 1976, pp. 34–39.

Jaslow, P. "Employment, Retirement and Morale Among Older Women." *Journal of Gerontology* 31, March 1976, pp. 212–218.

Kalich, Richard and Frances Knudtson. "Attachment vs. Disengagement: A Life-Span Conceptualization." *Human Development* 19 (1976), pp. 171–181.

Keyserling, M. D. "Economic Status of Women in the United States." *American Economic Review* 66, May 1976, pp. 205–212.

Kline, Chrysee. "The Socialization Process of Women: Implications for a Successful Theory of Aging." *Gerontologist* 15, Dec. 1975, pp. 486–492.

Koestenbaum, Peter. "The New Image of the Person: Loneliness, Love, Reality." Paper presented at Western Regional Meeting, Association for Humanistic Psychology, February 1979, pp. 1–20.

Landes, J. B. "Women, Labor and Family Life: A Theoretical Perspective." *Science and Society* 41, Winter 1977–1978, pp. 386–409.

Leacock, E. "Women's Status in Egalitarian Society: Implications for Social Evolution." *Current Anthropologist* 19, June 1978, pp. 247–275.

Lepper, Mary. "The Status of Women in the U.S., 1976: Still Looking for Justice and Equality." *Public Administration Review*, July/August 1976, pp. 365–368.

Leventhal, G. "Female Criminality: Is Women's Lib To Blame?" *Psychological Reporter* 41, Dec. 1977, pp. 1179–1182.

Levine, Adeline. "Women and the Fear of Success: A Problem in Replication." *American Journal of Sociology* 80, Jan. 1975, pp. 964–974.

Lieberman, M. A., and G. R. Bond. "Problems of Being a Woman: A Survey of 1700 Women in Consciousness-Raising Groups." *Journal of Applied Behavior Science* 12, No. 3 (1976), pp. 363–379.

Livson, Florence. "Patterns of Personality Development in Middle-Aged Women: A Longitudinal Study." *International Journal of Aging and Human Development* 7 (1976) pp. 107–115.

Lohmann, Nancy. "Correlations of Life Satisfaction, Morale, and Adjustment Measures." *Journal of Gerontology* 32, Jan. 1977, pp. 73–85.

Lowenthal, Marjorie F. and Lawrence Weiss. "Intimacy and Crisis in Adulthood." *Counseling Psychologist* 6 (1976), pp. 10–15.

Marecek, Jeanne and Diane Kravetz. "Women and Mental Health: A Review in Feminist Change Efforts." *Psychiatry* 40, Nov. 1977, pp. 561–590.

"Marital Role, Education and Mental Disorder Among Women." *Journal of Health and Social Behavior* 17, Sept. 1976, pp. 295–310.

Mason, K. O., *et al.* "Change in U.S. Women's Sex-Role Attitudes: 1964–1974." *American Sociology Review* 41, Aug. 1976, pp. 573–596.

McClelland, D. C. "Making It to Maturity." *Psychology Today* 12, June 1978, pp. 42–43.

Moslow, E. and P. Newberry. "Work Role and Depression in Women: A Comparison of Workers & Housewives in Treatment." *American Journal of Orthopsychiatry* 45, July 1975, pp. 538–547.

Moulton, R. "Some Effects of the New Feminism." *American Journal of Psychiatry* 134, Jan. 1977, pp. 1–6.

Nelson, L. B. "Social Standing of a Housewife." *Marriage and Family* 40, Aug. 1978, pp. 541–548.

Neugarten, Bernice. "Adaptation and the Life Cycles." *Counseling Psychologist* 6 (1976), pp. 16–20.

Nevill, Dorothy and Sandra Damico. "Developmental Components of Role Conflict in Women." *The Journal of Psychology* 95, March 1977, pp. 195–198.

Nydegger, Corinne. "Middle Age: Some Early Returns." *International Journal of Aging & Human Development* 7 (1976), pp. 131–141.

Olsen, N. J. and E. W. Willemsen. "Fear of Success: Fact or Artifact." *Journal of Psychology* 98, Jan. 1978, pp. 65–70.

Oppenheimer, V. K. "Sociology of Women's Economic Role in the Family." *American Sociological Review* 42, June 1977, pp. 387–406.

Ozawa, Martha. "Women and Work." *Social Work*, Nov. 1976, pp. 455–461.

Payne, Barbara and Frank Whittington. "Older Women: An Examination of Popular Stereotypes and Research Evidence." *Social Problems* 23, April 1976, pp. 488–501.

Pomerantz, Susan and William C. House. "Liberated Versus Traditional Women's Performance Satisfaction and Perceptions of Ability." *Journal of Psychology* 95, March 1977, pp. 205–211.

Powell, P. and M. Begnikoff. "Role Conflict and Symptoms of Psychological Distress in College-Educated Women." *Journal of Consulting Clinical Psychology* 44, June 1976, pp. 473–479.

Putnam, Leon J. "Venturing into Religious Maturity." *Intellect,* June 1978, pp. 487–488.

Roberts, Don. "Adult Life Cycles and Teaching." *The English Journal,* April 1978, pp. 14–17.

Rosenthal, S. F. "Female as Manipulator: A Replication." *Psychological Reporter* 42, Feb. 1978, pp. 151–158.

Rubin, Lillian. "Empty Nest: Empty Myth." *Psychology Today* 12, Dec. 1978, pp. 38+.

———. "Feminist Perspectives: The Sociological Challenge." *Social Problems* 23, April 1976, pp. 369–390.

Scarf, Maggie. "The More Sorrowful Sex." *Psychology Today* 12, April 1979, pp. 44+.

Schefland, Ellen and Elizabeth J. Koopman. "The Relationship of Women's Sex-Role Identity to Self-Esteem and Ego Development." *The Journal of Psychology* 98, March 1978, pp. 299–305.

Seal, H. "You've Come a Long Way, Baby: Fact, Fiction, or Myth." *Crises* 85, March 1978, pp. 102–104.

Seiden, Anne. "Overview: Research on the Psychology of Women. II. Women in Families, Work, and Psychotherapy." *American Journal of Psychiatry* 133, Oct. 1976, pp. 10+.

Sennott, Jan. D. "Sex-Role Inconstancy, Biology and Successful Aging." *Gerontologist* 17, Sept.-Oct. 1978, pp. 459–463.

"Special Issue on Women." *Social Work* 21, Nov. 1976, pp. 419–537.

Sprinthall, R. C., and B. Bennett. "Conformity and Non-Confor-

mity Among Married Women: The Reisman Typologies."
Psychological Reports, 1978, pp. 1195–1201.

Stein, Stefan, Stephen Holzman and Byram Karasu. "Mid-Adult Development and Psychopathology." *American Journal of Psychiatry* 135, June 1978, pp. 676–681.

Steward, Abigail. "How Women Cope with Stress—Contrasting Style." *Psychology Today,* June 1978, pp. 41+.

Stillion, Judith. "The Developmental Wheel." *Journal of Education* 7 (1975), pp. 11–16.

Stricker, G. "Implications of Research for Psychotherapeutic Treatment of Women." *American Psychologist* 32, Jan. 1977, pp. 14–22.

Strobber, M. H. "Wives' Labor Force Behavior and Family Consumption Patterns." *American Economic Review* 67, Feb. 1977, pp. 410–417.

Taylor, P. A. and N. D. Glenn. "Utility of Education and Attractiveness for Females: Status Attainment Through Marriage." *American Sociological Review* 41, Aug. 1976, pp. 573–596.

Troll, Lillian and Jean Smith. "Attachment Through the Life Span." *Human Development* 32, Jan. 1977, pp. 73–85.

Van Dusen, Roxann A. and Eleanor B. Sheldon. "Changing Status of American Women—A Life-Cycle Perspective." *American Psychologist* 31, Feb. 1976, pp. 106–116.

Vogel, S. R. "Sex-Role Self-Concepts and Life Style Plans of Young Women." *Journal of Consulting Clinical Psychology* 43, June 1975, pp. 427+.

Weinreich, H. "What Future for the Female Subject? Some Implications for the Women's Movement for Psychological Research." *Human Relations* 30, June 1977, pp. 535–543.

Winter, D. G., *et al.* "Husband's Motives and Wife's Career Level." *Journal of Personality and Social Psychology* 35, May 1977, pp. 159–166.

"Women and Change in the Developing World (Symposium)." *Journal of International Affairs* 30, Fall/Winter 1976–1977, pp. 151–268.

"Women and the Future—Symposium." *Futures* 7, Oct. 1975, pp. 362–435.

"Women in America—Symposium." *Current History* 70, May 1976, pp. 193–222.

Wright, J. D. "Are Working Women Really More Satisfied? Evidence from Several National Surveys." *American Political Science Review* 72, March 1978, pp. 135–150.